ANDY BULL is a keen walker, journalist and author who has written travel pieces for *The Times*, the *Daily Telegraph*, *The Independent*, the *Mail on Sunday* and *The Tablet*.

When he wanted to go on a pilgrimage that could be completed in a weekend, and found no suitable guides were available, he realised he would have to find a route for himself. He found 20, and *Pilgrim Pathways* is the result.

Andy has also published two travel books on America: *Coast to Coast* and *Strange Angels*; guides for mountain bikers to The Lake District and The Ridgeway; and *Walking Charles Dickens' Kent*. He has written the local history books *Secret Margate*; *Secret Ramsgate*; *Secret Broadstairs*; *Secret Twickenham, Whitton, Teddington and the Hamptons*; and *Secret Richmond*. He is now researching a book on the Great North Road.

Pilgrim Pathways – 1- 2 day walks on Britain's ancient sacred ways

First edition November 2020

Publisher Trailblazer Publications ● www.trailblazer-guides.com
The Old Manse, Tower Rd, Hindhead, Surrey, GU26 6SU, UK

British Library Cataloguing in Publication Data
A catalogue record for this book is available from the British Library

ISBN 978-1-912716-19-7

Text © Andy Bull 2020
Maps and diagrams © Trailblazer 2020

The right of Andy Bull to be identified as the author of this work has been
asserted by him in accordance with the Copyright, Designs and Patents Act 1988

Series Editor: Bryn Thomas   **Editor**: Nicky Slade
Layout: Bryn Thomas   **Cartography**: Nick Hill
Proofreading: Jane Thomas & Bryn Thomas   **Index**: Jane Thomas

Photographs © Andy Bull all photos except for:
p94 'Bodmin, St Petroc's ivory and gold casket' by Michael Garlick CC
p136 'St Mary's Mundon Interior' by Rwendland CC
p222 'Seahouses, Farne Islands' by Phil Sangwell CC
© Bryn Thomas (photos on p8 btm, p46 top & btm,
p47 top, p50 btm, p51 top R & btm, p52,
pp64-5 with permission of English Heritage, p109 btm)

Cover photo and pp78-9 'Glastonbury Tor'
© Robert Harding, Alamy Stock Photo

Photos – This page: Sheinton to Harley (Walk 14);
Previous page: After Tillingham (Walk 11); **Overleaf**: Elie Lady's Tower (Walk 20)

Important note

Every effort has been made by the author and publisher to ensure that the information
contained herein is as accurate and up to date as possible. However, they are unable to
accept responsibility for any inconvenience, loss or injury sustained by anyone
as a result of the advice and information given in this guide.

Printed in China; print production by D'Print (☎ +65-6581 3832), Singapore

Pilgrim Pathways

1-2 day walks on Britain's ancient sacred ways

ANDY BULL

TRAILBLAZER PUBLICATIONS

Contents

Contents

Author acknowledgements

There are several organisations and individuals championing the resurgence of pilgrimage in Great Britain, among them the British Pilgrimage Trust. I have on occasion taken inspiration from such pioneers, and would like to express my gratitude for their wonderful work.

I should stress, however, that each of the routes you see here has been adapted – often extensively – by me to fit my (largely) two-day pilgrimage format.

Walk 1 follows part of the route developed as the Way of St Augustine by Explore Kent.

Walk 2 takes inspiration from the Old Way developed by the British Pilgrimage Trust on the section from Battle to Winchelsea.

Walk 3 is adapted from The Jerusalem Pilgrimage created by William Parsons for the British Pilgrimage Trust.

Walk 7 follows the Cornwall Saints' Way, created by the Cooperative Retail Services Community Programme.

Walk 15 follows the Ebor Way, developed in the 1970s by the Ebor Acorn Rambling Club.

Walk 16 was inspired by the work of the Friends of Finchale Camino, who mapped out an English Camino pilgrim route. However, while my route takes in all of the pilgrim points they identify from Escomb to Finchale, I follow another path, the Weardale Way, between them in order to make this walk achievable in two days.

Walk 17 was inspired by the North Wales Pilgrim's Way, but only follows short stretches of the official path. I have extensively adapted the route, focusing on key pilgrim points, in order to make this achievable in three days – two if you are energetic enough.

Other walks are entirely my own invention.

Above: A misty morning walk near West Bexington, Dorset.

How to be a weekend pilgrim

If all you have to do to whistle is put your lips together and blow, then all you need to do to be a pilgrim is put one foot in front of the other. But where to? And why?

Many people are inspired by the idea of going on a pilgrimage. TV series such as *The Road to Rome* and *The Road to Santiago* have shown that even the averagely unfit celeb can hobble through one. However, few of the rest of us have time to walk Spain's Camino, the Via Francigena through France and Italy, or even the Pilgrims' Way from London to Canterbury. So what to do?

Pilgrim Pathways has the answer: 20 answers in fact. The pilgrimages in these pages are achievable for people with limited time and busy lives. The book was inspired by the belief that pilgrimage – variously defined as a journey on foot to a place that is holy, important or special – should be open to all.

There are many ancient pilgrim paths in Britain, some long-forgotten but recently rediscovered, others well-established – but all of them are dauntingly long. *Pilgrim Pathways* offers routes inspired by the very best of them, distilled into walks that can be accomplished comfortably in a weekend, and one would ideally suit a three-day break. I have also included suggestions for ways in which the routes can be divided into one-day sections, for times when you would rather not stay away overnight.

Why make a pilgrimage?

In pilgrimage, the journey itself is as important as the destination. Hence, these routes take in Britain's most inspiring landscapes and most powerfully spiritual places. They follow rivers, coastlines, forest tracks, and trails over hill and dale. They feature

Above: Holywell, North Wales.

Above: Following the lane through Fordwich on the Way of St Augustine, Kent.

cathedrals, ancient monasteries and churches, holy wells, wayside crosses, and other places of veneration: places that have paid mute witness to millennia of prayer.

Pilgrimage doesn't have to be traditionally religious in purpose, and some of these walks are rooted in prehistory, and our most powerful myths and legends. Pilgrimage to Avebury and Stonehenge, which features in Walk 4, dates back 5000 years. Glastonbury, in Walk 6, has its pilgrim roots in pre-Christian tales of Avalon and King Arthur.

Why you go is up to you. A pilgrimage can be approached through a desire to achieve inner peace, to defy an illness or condition, as a physical challenge, or simply to open up a breathing space in a busy life. If this coronavirus

pandemic has taught us anything, it is the value of being outside in the countryside and of taking care of our bodily and mental health. *Pilgrim Pathways* is designed to help you achieve your own personal goal.

But it shouldn't be too easy. Pilgrimage, to give a sense of achievement, of pushing your boundaries, should involve a significant physical challenge. To that end, these walks are designed to be vigorous for someone of average fitness, with some offering a greater degree of challenge than others.

Pilgrimage – an ancient tradition reclaimed

Once, before the Reformation, pilgrimage was very popular. Everyone aspired to go on at least one pilgrimage just as, today, all Muslims will hope to go to Mecca. Those who were incapable of getting to Canterbury, let alone to Rome or Jerusalem, could go on regional ones. Henry VIII ended all that. He made pilgrimage illegal, as part of a ban on the veneration of saints. In doing so he robbed his people of an ancient and hugely powerful tradition. Today, many are choosing to reclaim that tradition.

Above: A basket of pilgrim prayers in St David's Cathedral, Pembrokeshire.

Why did medieval pilgrims go? There were selfless motivations: to pay homage, to explore a mystery, and to travel in pursuit of enlightenment.

There were also purely selfish motives. Often, pilgrims wanted to be cured of an ailment. They were after miracles. The relics of the saints – their bodily remains – were believed to have great power. Pilgrims believed, for example, that the blood on the cloak of the murdered St Thomas Becket had healing properties. Holy wells such as St Winefride's Well in North Wales were also great draws, and it was believed their waters could cure a variety of ailments.

Many in the Church exploited the faith of pilgrims. They extorted and cheated them, promising rewards in the next life in return for financial offerings in this. Because a cathedral or a monastery needed a saint's relics to attract pilgrims – and the income they brought – relics were sometimes stolen or otherwise diverted to a site in need of them. In Walk 1 you'll read how St Mildred's bones were snaffled in the night from Minster on the Isle of Thanet and transferred to Canterbury, thereby forcing her pilgrims to divert to follow her.

Thankfully, there is no such skulduggery associated with modern pilgrimage.

Left: On the trail to Chichester Cathedral, West Sussex.

Planning your walk

The information for each walk comes from two sources – this book and the downloads accessible only to readers of this book from a web address given with each walk.

Choose your walk from this book

In the 20 sections of this book which follow, I recount my experience of each pilgrimage, a descriptive overview designed to give you an idea of the walk and to inspire you to do it. I give suggestions on where to stay, stop to eat, and generally how to plan your weekend or your day walk.

Choose your walk from the book, then go to the website page which has been created specifically to hold the downloads you'll find useful for navigation. The web page address is given in the practical information box of each walk in this book.

Downloadable practical information

On the website you'll find three files for each numbered walk:

● **.pdf file for paper-based walking instructions** This printable pdf file is a tabulated, step-by-step description, designed to be used in conjunction with the paper Ordnance Survey (OS) Explorer map listed in the book.

● **.gpx file for GPS route** If you have a smartphone with GPS capability (most modern phones have this) or a GPS unit (such as a Garmin) you can upload the relevant gpx file into the app used on it, and follow that as you walk. Each gpx file was recorded as I walked a given route, so should keep you exactly on the route, which will appear on your screen as a solid line.

If you're using the gpx file on your phone you'll need an app to load it into. I use the Ordnance Survey's app but there are several other apps that also use OS mapping.

● **.kml file for use with GoogleEarth** The GPS file is also supplied in that format. You can import it into GoogleEarth on your computer and make A4-sized screenshots of each birds-eye section of the walk which you could print out.

Note that you don't need all of these files to do the walks. If you prefer just using paper maps simply print the pdf file to use with your OS map.

I'm a belt, braces and possibly sock-suspenders sort of walker, so I use both the OS app and a paper map (using the gpx file and the pdf file). The app enables me to zoom in on my route, so I can see exactly – for example – which side of a hedge I should be walking along. That's great, but on its own is like looking at the route through a letterbox. So I carry the paper map in order to get an overview of the stretch I am tackling.

How to download the files from the website

These files on the internet do not appear on our public website as they are intended only for readers of this book. It is most important that you type the url directly into your browser. If you try to access it using a search engine (such as Google) it won't show up.

If, for example, you wish to get the files for Walk 18 you'll have seen in the practical information box the following:

- **Directions & GPS** 018.pdf, 018.gpx, 018.kml at 🖳 https://trailblazer-guides.com/press

Open your browser and type: https://trailblazer-guides.com/press into the browser to replace whichever website address the browser usually opens with. This will take you directly to the list of files on our website. Click on the required files to download them.

As explained above, there are three files for each walk: the **printable pdf file** with the walking and map directions, the **gpx file** if you're using gps navigation and the **kml file** if you want to see the route on GoogleEarth.

Getting to and from the walks

If you're doing the walks as day walks you'll need to use a bus, train or taxi at either the beginning or the end of the day as most of the walks are linear. There are various public transport apps but we've found **Rome2Rio** great for working out the best ways to and from a walk via public transport of all varieties.

If there are two or more of you on the walk and two cars you can of course park one at the end and then drive in the other to leave it at the start.

COVID-19

This book was partly researched during the coronavirus pandemic and even with the restrictions which that sometimes imposed it was nevertheless possible to do the walks and visit the shrines, chapels, churches and cathedrals along the routes. As we go to press all the places to stay and places to eat mentioned are still trading.

1 The Way of St Augustine
Ramsgate to Canterbury
19.2 miles/31km

Journey from St Augustine's shrine at Ramsgate through the watery world of the Stour Valley to the saint's abbey and cathedral at Canterbury, and the heart of English Christianity. St Augustine arrived in Kent in 597AD, on a mission from Pope Gregory to bring Christianity to southern England. Close to the point at which he came ashore, Ebbsfleet on the Isle of Thanet, is St Augustine's Cross, which marks the point at which he first preached on English soil and met the Kentish King Ethelbert.

Beginning on the Ramsgate clifftops, along the way you take in quiet orchards, the wonderfully bird-rich water meadows and marshes of Stodmarsh National Nature Reserve, and Saxon places of worship.

2 The Old Way to the Fifth Continent
Battle, Rye, and four Romney Marsh churches *27.6 miles/44.5km*

Follow a long-forgotten pilgrim path from William the Conqueror's victory altar at Battle Abbey to Romney Marsh, and a clutch of simple, ancient churches set in a stark landscape.

The middle of a battlefield is not an obvious place to begin a pilgrimage but, at Battle, where William defeated Harold in 1066, it makes sense. The Conqueror built a great abbey at the site of his victory, placing the altar on the exact spot Harold was killed.

Battle is also on a medieval pilgrim path. Canterbury-bound pilgrims from Southampton followed the High Weald to this abbey, and on to Winchelsea and Rye. You'll be travelling through a varied and beautiful landscape, from gently undulating farmland and woods before a steep climb onto the downs, then down to level river- and canal-side walking before arriving at the flat, exposed Romney Marsh.

3 Blake, Jerusalem and St Richard
Haslemere to Chichester
25.4 miles/40.9km

This route follows St Richard's pilgrim path through the West Sussex landscape that inspired William Blake to write a poem, *And Did Those Feet In Ancient Time*, which later became better-known as *Jerusalem*.

Beginning in the Surrey Hills, you take in the far-reaching views from the evocatively named Temple of the Winds before continuing on towards the historic West Sussex market town of Midhurst. The beauty of the South Downs leads you to the Trundle, an ancient holy hill, before descending to Chichester and the Guildhall where Blake was tried and acquitted of the capital offences of treason and sedition, finishing at Chichester cathedral.

(cont'd on p16)

Pilgrim Pathways

Rail at start/end	Miles/Km		Ascent	Types of terrain & Level of difficulty
Ramsgate/Canterbury	19.2	31	640m/2099ft	Grass/earth paths *Easy*
Battle/Appledore	27.6	44.5	682m/2237ft	Grass/earth paths, woodland paths *Moderate to challenging*
Haslemere/ Chichester	25.4	40.9	1375m/4510ft	Grass/earth paths, woodland tracks *Moderate*
Swindon/Salisbury	26.9	43.3	926m/2745ft	Grass/paths, rough tracks, lanes *Challenging*
Weymouth/Axminster	22.9	36.9	1892m/6207	Cliff grass/paths, beach, pavements *Mainly moderate, challenging stretches*
Worle/Castle Cary	22	35.5	1210m/3970ft	Grass/paths, woodland tracks, lanes *Mainly moderate, challenging stretches*
Bodmin Parkway/Par	27.6	44.4	1329m/4359ft	Grass/paths, farm tracks, quiet lanes *Challenging*
Haverfordwest	19.8	31.8	1057m/3466ft	Rocky coastal paths *Challenging*
Didcot Parkway/Oxford	20.6	33.2	379m/1241ft	Grass/earth paths, towpath *Easy*
Westminster/Marble Arch	9.9	16	Negligible	Pavements *Easy*
Chelmsford/Southminster	16.6	26.7	99.8m/328ft	Grass/earth paths *Easy*
Thetford/Bury St Edm	18.9	30.4	193m/632ft	Grass/paths, forest tracks, pavement *Easy*
Kings Lynn	21.4	34.4	263m/865ft	Grass/earth paths, quiet lanes *Moderate*
Telford	14.8	23.8	607m/1990ft	Grass/paths, farm tracks, quiet lanes *Easy, with moderate stretch climbing Wenlock Edge*
Leeds/York	21.1	33.9	253m/830ft	Grass/earth paths *Easy*
Bishop Auckland/Durham	20.7	33.3	600m/1970ft	Grass/riverbank paths, pavements *Easy*
Flint/Llanrwst	33	53.1	1609m/5278ft	Grass/earth paths, quiet lanes *Challenging*
Danby/Whitby	19.3	31.1	828m/2716ft	Grass/paths, packhorse routes, tracks *Moderate*
Chathill/Berwick	22.2	35.7	550m/1869ft	Beach, paths, quiet lanes, causeway *Moderate*
Markinch/Leuchars	25.1	40.5	848m/2782ft	Grass/coast path, sandy/rocky beaches *Challenging*

4 A prehistoric pilgrimage
Avebury to Stonehenge
26.9 miles/43.3km

This pre-Christian pilgrimage through the Avebury and Stonehenge UNESCO World Heritage Site follows an ancient ceremonial route along the valley of the River Avon.

Avebury has the largest megalithic stone circle in the world. The three circles are 5000 years old and are believed to have been used in ritual or ceremony. Stonehenge has been a place of pilgrimage for millennia. It is believed the two were linked by a pilgrim route that took its followers on a symbolic journey through life to death. Today it takes you on a fairly stiff hike via an exposed Neolithic burial mound, over Salisbury Plain and on through a string of riverside villages before the final approach towards Stonehenge along the most ancient of pilgrim paths.

5 A Jurassic Coast pilgrimage
Abbotsbury, Chideock, Whitchurch Canonicorum and Lyme Regis
22.9 miles/36.9km

Walking this spectacular coastline takes you from the lonely hill-top chapel of St Catherine, patron saint of single women, via the Catholic Martyrs' church at Chideock and the ancient shrine of St Wite at Whitchurch Canonicorum, to Lyme Regis. Some strenuous climbing is amply rewarded with panoramic views from the highest point on the Jurassic coast at Golden Cap.

6 The path to Avalon
The pilgrim route to Wells and Glastonbury
22 miles/35.5km

You'll be riding the rolling Mendips through nature reserves and limestone crags to the holy wells of Wells and its remarkable cathedral. From there it's on across the wide-open Somerset Levels to Glastonbury, where legends of Jesus and King Arthur combine.

You climb Glastonbury Tor, a vertiginous hill rising from the Somerset Levels, topped by St Michael's tower, which may be the Isle of Avalon in Arthurian legend. Finally you descend to visit Chalice Well, one of Britain's most ancient wells, and Glastonbury Abbey, founded in the 7th century and associated with the legends of the Holy Grail and King Arthur. There is a legend that Joseph of Arimathea brought the boy Jesus here, leading to the belief by some that Glastonbury is the cradle of English Christianity.

7 The Cornish Saints' Way
Coast to coast, Padstow to Fowey
27.6 miles/44.4km

Celtic saints and pilgrims crossed Cornwall on their way from Wales and Ireland to Spain and the Compostela pilgrimage, avoiding the treacherous sea journey around Land's End. This route takes you coast to coast, across wild moorland and sheltered valleys, taking in Celtic crosses, shrines to obscure Celtic saints and holy wells along the way.

8 The Path of St David
A coastal pilgrimage through a sacred landscape *19.8 miles/31.8km*

With the sea as your constant companion, you'll be walking in the footsteps of Wales's patron saint, from St David's baptism on St Elvis Farm to the ancient chapel and holy well of his mother, St Non, and the cathedral in the town that bears his name. St David's Cathedral stands on the site of the monastery he founded in the coastal valley of Glyn Rhosyn in Pembrokeshire and has been a major place of pilgrimage for 1200 years.

9 A Thames pilgrimage
Dorchester to Abingdon, Oxford and Binsey *20.6 miles/3.2km*

Four saints, a sacred river, and the shrine and holy well where Henry VIII's first wife Catherine of Aragon came to pray for a son make for a peaceful pilgrimage with plenty of time for contemplation. Walking through open countryside into the heart of Oxford and beyond, you'll get a very different perspective on the venerable River Thames.

10 London's saints and martyrs
Westminster Abbey to Tyburn *9.9 miles/16km*

A sacred-London pilgrimage, walking in the footsteps of St Edward the Confessor and St Botolph, patron saint of travellers; touching the holy marks left by martyrs in the Tower of London; and visiting the greatest abbey and cathedral. You'll also echo the final journey of those condemned to death, through city streets thronged with onlookers, via St Giles-in-the-Fields and down Oxford Street to the gallows at Tyburn Tree. On the way they were allowed a last drink at The Angel pub, still in existence today.

11 St Peter's Way
Across the Essex marshes to St Peter-on-the-Wall *16.6 miles/26.7km*

St Peter-on-the-Wall is an ancient Saxon chapel built by St Cedd on the shore-side ruins of a Roman fort in 654AD. You'll travel along St Peter's Way, a 1300-year-old pilgrims' route via remote villages and ancient churches, encompassing a network of tidal creeks, mudflats and salt marsh that offer a bird-watcher's paradise.

12 St Edmund's Way
Thetford to Bury St Edmunds *18.9 miles/30.4km*

In the 13th and 14th centuries the Priory of Our Lady of Thetford was a significant destination for pilgrims, with a statue of the Virgin that was said to perform miracles. Setting off from Thetford offers a varied backdrop to your walk, from riverside through forest and along quiet lanes as well as open countryside, before arriving at Bury St Edmund's Abbey, the ruins of which are alongside the city's cathedral. It attracted pilgrims as it was the burial place of the Anglo-Saxon martyr-king St Edmund, killed by the Danes in 869.

13 England's Nazareth
Castle Acre to Walsingham
21.4 miles/34.8km

Beginning in Castle Acre, the walk takes in quiet country lanes via a Saxon round-tower church and the curious, long-abandoned medieval village of Godwick, following the final stage of the old pilgrim route from London to Walsingham. Here in 1061, noblewoman Lady Richeldis built a richly decorated replica of the Holy Family's house, which became a shrine and attracted pilgrims to Walsingham from all over Europe. Although completely obliterated during the Dissolution, the site of the shrine is marked in the grounds of the ruined Walsingham Abbey. Pilgrimage has now been revived, and there are Anglican, Catholic and Orthodox shrines in the village. The Catholic shrine is in the Slipper Chapel, a mile from the Holy House, where pilgrims would leave their shoes and continue barefoot.

14 St Milburga's Shropshire
Ironbridge, Much Wenlock, Wenlock Edge
14.8 miles/23.8km

This circular route takes you from Ironbridge, birthplace of the Industrial Revolution, via the riverside Buildwas Abbey, and ascends the dramatic 1000ft limestone escarpment of Wenlock Edge before dropping down to Much Wenlock. Wenlock Priory, or St Milburga's Priory, is thought to be the final resting place of the 8th century abbess St Milburga. Her shrine and St Milburga's Well, which was believed to cure eye diseases, were great pilgrimage sites until the Reformation.

15 St Paulinus and the Ebor Way
Wetherby to York
21.1 miles/33.9km

The route shadows two rivers and the course of a Roman road from Wetherby to York, following the Ebor Way, from Eboracum, the Roman name for York. It was travelled by St Paulinus, a young Roman monk who, in 601, was sent to convert the northern Britons to Christianity and later became the first Bishop of York. The half-way point is Tadcaster where, coincidentally, the Pilgrim Fathers decided to set sail for America. The River Ouse leads you right into the heart of York, where you'll be rewarded with the spectacle of York Minster, the largest Gothic cathedral in northern Europe.

16 The English Camino
Escomb to Finchale Priory via Durham   *20.7 miles/33.3km*

Strike out on the route travelled by St Oswald, one of the first English pilgrims to walk the Spanish Camino to Santiago. It begins at the village of Escomb, which has one of the most complete Saxon churches in England. With the River Wear as your constant companion you'll arrive in the great city of Durham to visit St Oswald's church, St Oswald's Well and Durham Cathedral, with its shrine to St Cuthbert.

This is part of a recognised English section of the Camino de Santiago, which starts at the port cities of A Coruna and Ferrol, at which medieval pilgrims arrived from England.

17 The Welsh Lourdes and the Burial Place of Saints

From Basingwerk Abbey via Holywell to Gwytherin *33 miles/53.1km*

For those who relish a physical challenge, this section of the North Wales Pilgrim's Way offers plenty of climbing and descending with impressive views. It takes in St Winefride's Well at Holywell, which claims to be the oldest continually visited place of pilgrimage in Britain. Almost uniquely for places of veneration, it survived the Reformation, perhaps due to its close connections with generations of Tudor royalty.

St Winefride was a 7th century Christian woman of royal lineage who was murdered by a prince for rejecting his advances. She spent much of her later life in the Conwy village of Gwytherin, where she was buried. The chapel built over her open grave is long gone, but in 1896 a new church was built in the village, dedicated to Winefride, and is now a civil wedding venue surrounded by an ancient Celtic saints' burial ground.

18 St Hilda and the Blessed Nicholas Postgate

Danby to Whitby *19.3 miles/31.1km*

Strike out along the Esk Valley on the trail of a saint and the martyred priest of the moors. Walking the North York moors rewards you with far-reaching views from Danby Beacon. Along the way, at Egton Bridge the path coincides with memorials to the Blessed Nicholas Postgate. Born in Egton in 1596, Postgate risked his life by preaching illegally in secret locations across a wide area and was eventually caught and executed.

The walk ends with a wonderful descent into Whitby, and the ruins of St Hilda's abbey. St Hilda was an Anglo-Saxon princess and abbess of Whitby Abbey who, in 664, hosted the Synod of Whitby at which decisions were made that ended the sway of the Irish monks of Iona in favour of Roman Catholicism.

19 St Cuthbert, St Oswald and St Aidan

Seahouses to Holy Island, Northumberland *22.2 miles/35.7km*

The walk from Seahouses via Bamburgh to Holy Island follows the footsteps of three revered Northern Saints: St Cuthbert, who travelled via Seahouses to his retirement home on the Farne Islands; St Oswald, king of Northumbria, for whom Bamburgh Castle was a fortress home; and St Aidan, to whom Oswald gave the island of Lindisfarne (Holy Island) to found a monastery and Christianise his people. Accessible only at low tide, the causeway across to Holy Island offers a unique pilgrimage experience little changed in many hundreds of years.

20 St Andrew's Way

On the Fife Costal Path from Earlsferry to St Andrews *25.1 miles/40.5km*

From the 12th century pilgrims followed this and other routes to the shrine of St Andrew in the city that bears his name. This exhilarating walk demands careful planning and awareness of the tide times, as the path takes you along rugged coastline via hermits' caves, holy wells and charming fishing villages.

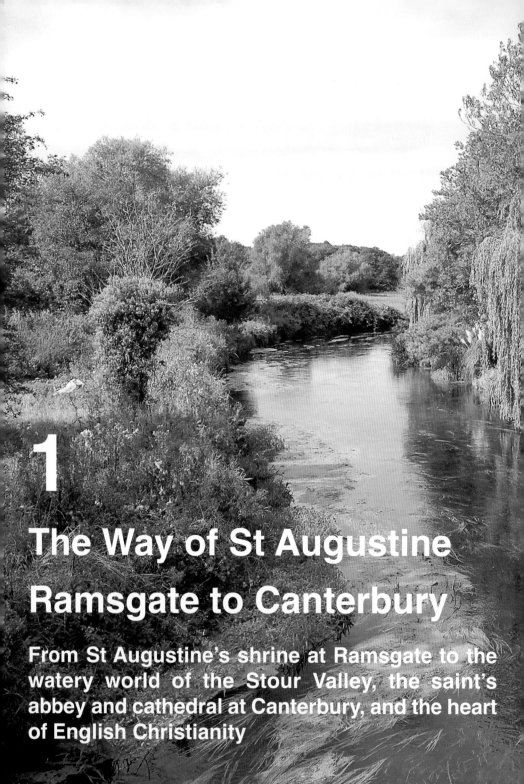

1

The Way of St Augustine
Ramsgate to Canterbury

From St Augustine's shrine at Ramsgate to the watery world of the Stour Valley, the saint's abbey and cathedral at Canterbury, and the heart of English Christianity

Every pilgrim deserves a little good fortune. I happen to have chosen two September days which prove to be the last gasp of summer for my pilgrimage along The Way of St Augustine. The sun is sparkling on Pegwell Bay as I look out from the clifftop church in Ramsgate that bears the saint's name.

Ahead of me, blessed by sun and gentle breezes, is a wonderful walk up the Stour Valley, beside reed-fringed rivers, through wildlife-rich water meadows, visiting isolated Saxon churches, remote hamlets and country pubs on my way to the World Heritage Site at Canterbury, with its triple crown of St Martin's church, St Augustine's Abbey and Canterbury Cathedral.

Soon I will be rounding the headland to the west and dipping down to what was once the mouth of the Wantsum – the channel that separated this Isle of Thanet from the Kent mainland – and St Augustine's Cross. Here it was that Augustine, arriving in 597AD on his mission from Rome to bring Christianity to England, met the King of Kent, Ethelbert. From there, the then-pagan king appeased, Augustine was able to travel by boat up the Wantsum and into the River Stour, which took him to Canterbury. This pilgrimage follows in his footsteps, but on the dry land that has replaced the watery world he encountered.

For centuries, St Augustine has been something of a forgotten saint, but in recent years his central place in England's religious and cultural history has been marked formally. In 2012, a new shrine was dedicated to him, housing a relic: a fragment of bone that is one of the few surviving pieces of his body. Yet the new shrine is not in Canterbury. It is here in Ramsgate.

The Great Stour at Fordwich

PRACTICAL INFORMATION

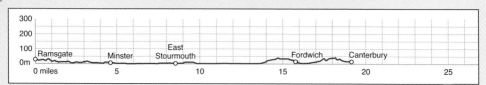

- **Terrain** Largely flat grass paths with one section along a fast road with no pavement
- **Difficulty** Easy
- **Directions & GPS*** 001.pdf, 001.gpx, 001.kml at 🖳 https://trailblazer-guides.com/press

See p10-11 for more information on downloads

ROUTE OVERVIEW   19.2 miles (31km)

The start and end points of this walk are easily accessed by public transport and there are several good lunch options en route. Pick up a Pilgrim Passport at the Shrine of St Augustine before you set off.

Ramsgate to East Stourmouth   9.2 miles (14.8km)

- **Time** 3hrs 30mins actual walking time
- **Total ascent** 334m/1095ft
- **Map** OS Explorer *150 Canterbury & Isle of Thanet*

From St Augustine's Shrine in Ramsgate you pick up the official Way of St Augustine footpath and follow it over flat terrain to the village of Minster **(4.7 miles)**, with its priory, then walk along the River Stour, departing from the official Way of St Augustine route shortly before Plucks Gutter, reached after a further **3.5miles**. At Plucks Gutter you leave the river for the village of East Stourmouth **(1 mile)**.

East Stourmouth to Canterbury   10 miles (16.2km)

- **Time** 3hrs 45mins actual walking time
- **Total ascent** 306m/1004ft
- **Map** OS Explorer *150 Canterbury & Isle of Thanet*

First it's a short stretch **(0.7 miles)** through apple orchards to West Stourmouth, then back to the riverside and the Way of St Augustine again. A peaceful walk follows, through the bird-rich water meadows and marshes of the Stodmarsh National Nature Reserve, before you reach the village of Stodmarsh, in **4.3 miles**. From Stodmarsh you follow the Stour Valley Walk through gently undulating pasture to Fordwich, after **2.7 miles,** then return to the Way of St Augustine through woodland to Canterbury **(2.3 miles)**.

Day walk options

For a greater challenge complete the whole walk in a day, or start from East Stourmouth.
- **By public transport** There are railway stations in both Ramsgate and Canterbury. To start from East Stourmouth, take a train to Minster and a bus or taxi to East Stourmouth.
- **Taxi option** Canterbury Taxis (☎ 01227 444444, 🖳 canterburytaxis.co.uk)

Where to eat or stay along the way

● **Ramsgate** Stay in a sea-view room at the *Royal Harbour Hotel*, (☎ 01843-591514, 🖥 royalharbour hotel.co.uk, 10 Nelson Cres) a five-minute walk from the starting point.

● **Minster** For **lunch** choose either modern British cuisine at the *Corner House Hotel* (☎ 01843-823000, 🖥 cornerhouserestaurants.co.uk; noon-2.30 & 6-9pm) or the hearty pub grub of *The Bell Inn* (☎ 01843-825707, 🖥 thebellinnminster.weebly.com; noon-midnight).

● **East Stourmouth** Stay at cosy village inn *The Rising Sun* (☎ 01227-721364, 🖥 the risingsunstourmouth.co.uk; food 12-2.30pm, 6.30-9.30pm).

● **Fordwich** Eat lunch at either the Michelin-starred *Fordwich Arms* (☎ 01227-710444, 🖥 fordwicharms.co.uk; noon-10.30pm) or the *George and Dragon* (☎ 01227-710661, 🖥 brunningandprice.co.uk/georgeand dragon; noon-9pm) both on King Street.

● **Canterbury** has a wide choice of places to stay and eat.

PILGRIMAGE HIGHLIGHTS

● Pick up a **Pilgrim Passport** in Pugin's gothic masterpiece, the **Shrine of St Augustine** (🖥 augustine-pugin.org.uk; 10am-4pm, St Augustine's Rd) and have it stamped along the way at **St Mary the Virgin, Minster**; **All Saints**, **West Stourmouth**, (both 10am-4pm) and **St Mary the Virgin, Fordwich** (10am-3pm)

● Take the **tour** of **Minster Abbey, St Mildred's Priory,** home of nuns who escaped Nazi Germany, and maybe join them for midday prayers (🖥 minsterabbey nuns.org; tours Sat 11am-noon).

● In **Canterbury**, visit the three pilgrim sites of **St Martin's** church (🖥 martin paul.org, North Holmes Rd), **St Augustine's Abbey** (Apr-Sept 10am-6pm, Oct to 5pm, Nov-Mar to 4pm), and **Canterbury Cathedral** (🖥 canterbury-cathedral.org; Sun 9am-4.30pm, winter 10am-4.30pm) each of which has a pilgrim stamp. At the cathedral, it is in the visitors' centre.

● Complete your pilgrimage with a blessing at the Cathedral, and maybe attend **Choral Evensong** (daily 5.30pm).

St Augustine's feast day: 26 May

The Shrine of St Augustine, Ramsgate

Arriving at this austere, glowering-black, knapped-flint church on the cliff top you might wonder why it is that the national Shrine to St Augustine should be tucked away here, in this rather faded seaside town. Only when you experience the splendour inside does it make sense. The 19th century architect Augustus Welby Northmore Pugin built this church, and dedicated it to his patron saint. Alongside it he built himself a house, The Grange, from which he could look down on St Augustine's landing point at Cliffs End.

Pugin, best known for designing the sumptuous Gothic Revival interiors of the Houses of Parliament, and the Elizabeth Tower that closets Big Ben, was a Catholic convert with a passionate desire to re-establish the religious practices and architectural styles of pre-Reformation England, and the church he built here is an embodiment of those beliefs.

Step inside, and you discover an extraordinary enclosed world. The church – which Pugin referred to as his own child – is approached along the three enfolding sides of a covered cloister. The north houses the

Above: Church of the Shrine of St Augustine, beside Pugin's house. **Below**: Stations of the Cross.

THE *ORIGINAL* CANTERBURY PILGRIMAGE

This Canterbury pilgrimage is 600 years older than the one Chaucer wrote about. His pilgrims followed the North Downs east through Kent, and came to venerate Thomas Becket, the archbishop and 'turbulent priest' murdered in his cathedral in 1170 by knights loyal to Henry II, with whom he was in a power struggle. Yet, in the six centuries before Becket's murder, it was St Augustine who brought pilgrims to Canterbury.

Becket's cult was snuffed out in 1538 by Henry VIII's relentless campaign to smash the shrines of all saints, destroy the marks of veneration, scatter the relics, and put a stop to pilgrimage. St Augustine's shrine, in the abbey he established close to his cathedral, was also destroyed. Henry's desecration robbed his people of not just a tradition, but the fulfilment of a deep-felt need: to pay homage, to explore a mystery, and to travel in pursuit of enlightenment.

stations of the cross: 14 vivid scenes from Christ's final journey to crucifixion; and what an extraordinary, three-dimensional, technicolour extravaganza it is.

With each turn of the cloister you are drawn gently towards the final, theatrical reveal: the church itself. Before you is the octagonal Caen stone font (**photo below**),

its canopy a soaring, remarkably delicate tracery in oak that towers to the very ceiling. Beside it is the Shrine to St Augustine: a deep red and sage green canopied reliquary.

To the right of that is the Pugin Chantry chapel, containing the architect's tomb, where he is buried. The stained-glass window depicts scenes from St Augustine's life, and lays out the key points on the pilgrimage you are just beginning: his landing; preaching to King Ethelbert; processing with his monks to Canterbury; saying mass at St Martin's church; baptising

Ethelbert; and laying the foundation stone for St Augustine's Abbey.

It's time to get walking, but first pick up a Pilgrim Passport (**photo left**) in which to collect stamps along the route.

St Augustine's Cross

The walk follows the clifftop out of town. You round Pegwell Bay and strike inland to Cliffs End where, on Cottington Road, a Celtic stone cross stands behind a fence. This is St Augustine's Cross, erected in 1884 to mark the spot at which Augustine met King Ethelbert, and preached his first sermon on English soil in 597AD.

Christianity was a minority faith in Roman times and almost disappeared after their departure. Bertha, Ethelbert's queen, was a Christian from France, and Augustine knew he could expect a sympathetic hearing. If Augustine could convert the king, the people of Kent would follow.

The cross (**photo left**) was erected at the spot where a tree called St Augustine's Oak had stood until the 19th century. It is sited in Cottmanfield, whose original meaning was 'field of the man of God'.

St Mildred's Priory (Minster Abbey)

There is a remarkable story of renewal at the next stop, Minster Abbey; a place where the rhythms of an ancient way of life once again resonate.

For many centuries Minster Abbey suffered: sacked by Vikings and Danes, half-demolished at the Reformation and sold as a private house. And then came a second

THE THEFT OF THE BONES OF ST MILDRED

St Mildred was attracting so many pilgrims to Minster that, in 1031, it was decided by the then Abbot of St Augustine's Abbey, Canterbury, to dedicate a shrine to her there, and transfer her remains to it. According to the 13th century *Life of Mildred* (anon), her removal was intended to be carried out in secret, but: 'The people of Thanet, happening to hear of the monks' doings, gave chase ... arming themselves with swords and staves and weapons of all sorts, to recover the body of their glorious Saint. But the monks had a fair start; and when the angry multitude first sighted them, they had already secured the ferry boats at Sarre, and were rowing swiftly over the broad waters of the Wantsum.'

To complete the circle, in 1963 a relic of St Mildred was brought here from Holland and enshrined in a new altar in the chapel.

flowering. In 1937, Benedictine nuns from Bavaria were confronted with the rise of the Nazi regime when the SS requisitioned part of their property. On the same day the abbess heard that the former abbey at Minster was for sale. She saw the hand of providence in this coincidence and, against huge odds, managed to raise the funds to buy it and escape here. The sisters set about healing the fractured history of the place that was their salvation, and dedicated the abbey to St Mildred, who was abbess in the 8th century.

Below: St Mildred's Priory, Minster Abbey.

Above: Minster – outside the church of St Mary.

Ancient though Minster Abbey is, it was originally established in 670AD at our second pilgrim-point in Minster, where the **church of St Mary the Virgin** now stands. The church, established here after the nuns outgrew the site, has Saxon elements but was enlarged by the Normans. The stunning nave, unchanged since 1150, has earned it the title The Cathedral of the Marshes. You can stamp your pilgrim passport here, before taking the zig-zag route across the fields to the banks of the River Stour.

The gentle amble beside the reed-fringed, swan-patrolled river is one of the most enjoyable stretches of the walk. At Plucks Gutter, where the river once met the sea, the route tacks inland to East Stourmouth and the suggested overnight stay at the Rising Sun.

The Saxon pilgrim churches of the Stour Valley

As you walk through the apple orchards from East to West Stourmouth, the shingles of a little spire and bell tower poking above the churchyard yews announce All Saints, the first of two lovely pilgrim churches.

Inside is a sacred space where mote-flecked shafts of sunlight penetrate the stained glass, made inexpertly by a rector in the 19th century, and give the box pews a subtle glow. From the wall above the little organ, with its brightly painted pipes, a board bears a wonderfully wise prayer, which asks: 'Give me neither poverty, nor riches, feed me with food convenient for me: Lest I be full, and deny thee, and say: 'Who is the Lord? or lest I be poor and steal, and take the name of my God in vain.' (*Proverbs, Ch 30, Ve 9*).

Below, left: Plucks Gutter.   **Right**: All Saints Church, West Stourmouth.

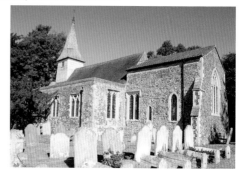

Here, the Stour is two rivers. From West Stourmouth you pass briefly alongside the Little Stour before crossing the fields to join its bigger, wetter brother, the Great Stour. Past Grove Ferry, you go up the Stour Valley and through the Stodmarsh National Nature Reserve. Here the lakes, reed beds and marshy grassland are home to otters, water voles, crayfish, kingfishers and snipe. You emerge at the village of Stodmarsh, beside its church, St Mary's, where crusaders on their way to the Holy Land stopped to pray. They scratched crosses into the stone doorframe, beseeching divine protection.

Fordwich and St Augustine

There is a long woodland stretch, through a remnant of a once extensive forest, before the next village, Fordwich. Its church, St Mary the Virgin, holds a mysterious Romanesque tomb, carved with a series of pillars along the sides and tiles on the pitched dome. Could this have been St Augustine's? It could, according to local legend.

The church guidebook says: 'It may have been part of his original tomb, or it may be all that is left of a shrine that pilgrims will have visited to offer prayers in his name... St Augustine may have died in the nearby infirmary of his monastery and may have been laid out here before being translated to the cathedral.'

At the foot of the church tower is a wooden shelf, where you will find the stamp for your pilgrim passport. In the 16th and 17th centuries it was known as the Bread Shelf: worshippers who could spare bread would leave it here for the poor.

The river at Fordwich really deserves to be contemplated before moving on. From the garden of the George and Dragon by the bridge I watch the languid, bream-rich, bottle-green waters glide by. From Fordwich it is just a short walk in dappled light through ancient woodlands to Canterbury and our next pilgrim point: the little church of St Martin.

St Martin's – the oldest church in the English-speaking world

Christian worship has taken place at St Martin's – tucked away on a yew-sheltered mound as you enter Canterbury – for 1400 years. This, remarkably, is the oldest church in continuous use in the English-speaking world. It was here that Ethelbert's Christian queen Bertha worshipped, and where Augustine and his monks came to pray and carry out their pastoral work while their abbey was being built nearby.

Ethelbert, who had brought Augustine to Canterbury because it was his capital, funded the building of his monastery and

Below, left: A possible tomb of St Augustine's at Fordwich.   **Right**: St Martin's, Canterbury.

endowed it with land – including the stretch you walked through today – so it was financially independent.

The church has been heavily rebuilt, but its earliest parts date from the 4th century, including the wall to the right of the simple, and very affecting, statue of Queen Bertha, in dark wood with gold crown and cross-embossed bible.

St Augustine's Abbey

The abbey is physically the least impressive of the three Canterbury sites. Little remains of it above ground level, so if you find the ruins uninspiring, focusing instead on its religious and cultural significance helps to put the site into perspective.

This was the first monastery founded in England, in 598AD. It would remain an important spiritual and cultural centre for a thousand years. Initially there were three small churches here, including one dedicated to St Peter and St Paul, where Augustine was first buried, as were Ethelbert and Bertha. A cult had been building around St Augustine since his death in 604, and in 1091 his remains were transferred to a glorious shrine at the east end of a new Norman church, which became a great place of pilgrimage. That changed after the death of Thomas Becket, when pilgrims came instead to venerate him, at his shrine in Canterbury cathedral.

Canterbury Cathedral

It is a short walk from the abbey up Burgate to the cathedral. The heart of this place for pilgrims is The Martyrdom, an

Below: The ruins of St Augustine's Abbey with Canterbury Cathedral in the background.

area down a flight of stone steps to the left of the Quire. Here it was that, at dusk on 29 December 1170, knights loyal to Henry II hacked Becket down. He had been preparing for *vespers* (evening prayers) when he was attacked. He was declared a saint three years after his murder.

From The Martyrdom you can descend to the 11th century crypt, where Becket's original shrine stood. Here, Antony Gormley's astonishing sculpture *Transport*, a male form created from nails originally used in the cathedral roof, appears to float in space. It is as if a hologram of a man has been moulded from a crown of thorns.

In 1220 a new gold, bejewelled shrine was created for Becket. His cult was one that questioned the king's supremacy in Church matters, and so attracted particular venom from Henry VIII, who ordered the shrine to be completely obliterated. Symbolically, a sole candle now marks the spot where it once stood, reached by climbing to emerge in Trinity Chapel.

Four years after the murder, and within a year of Becket's elevation to sainthood, a now penitent Henry II came here. He walked through Canterbury barefoot and, at Becket's tomb, was whipped by each of five bishops and 100 monks. You don't need to go that far. Instead, you can receive a blessing.

Pilgrims are greeted with great enthusiasm at the cathedral and encouraged to ask the priest who will be on duty beside the pulpit to bless them, and their journey. The Revd Bill Hornsby does the honours for me. Once blessed, I feel my first pilgrimage is truly complete.

Below: The Martyrdom, Canterbury Cathedral.

2

The Old Way
to the Fifth Continent

Battle, Rye and four
Romney Marsh churches

Following a long-forgotten pilgrim path from William the
Conqueror's victory altar at Battle to Romney Marsh,
and a clutch of lonely churches

The middle of a battlefield is not an obvious place to begin a pilgrimage but, at Battle, where William defeated Harold in 1066, it makes sense. The Conqueror built a great abbey at the site of his victory, placing the altar on the exact spot Harold was killed, and endowing it with what he believed were sacred relics of Christ, including parts of his manger and swaddling, as well as portions of the True Cross and the Holy Sepulchre.

In doing so he sought to make the place of his victory the most holy spot in this conquered kingdom. The abbey church is gone, but a stone marks the place where, legend has it, an arrow pierced Harold's eye.

Why did William mark his victory in this way? In penance for the blood shed in battle? To give thanks to God? To create a monument to his triumph? Whatever his motivation, this, the site of the most significant battle in English history, is a place for a pilgrim to pause for thought, because the Normans, in their unparalleled campaign of church and cathedral building, founded or re-shaped so many of the sacred places you will visit on this and other pilgrimages.

Battle is also on a medieval pilgrim path. Canterbury-bound pilgrims from Southampton followed the High Weald to this abbey, and on to Winchelsea and Rye, a route that is being revived under the name The Old Way.

Site of the altar marking the spot where Harold was killed.

PRACTICAL INFORMATION

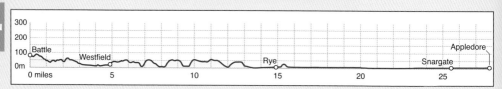

- **Terrain** Grass and woodland paths, sustained climb and sharp descent on Battle to Rye section; completely flat on Rye to Appledore section
- **Difficulty** Moderate to challenging
- **Directions & GPS*** 002.pdf, 002.gpx, 002.kml at 🖳 https://trailblazer-guides.com/press
  * See p10-11 for more information on downloads

ROUTE OVERVIEW   27.6 miles (44.5km)

Taking in parts of the 1066 Country Walk and the Saxon Shore Way, the steep climb up to Icklesham is well worth the effort for the fabulous views.

Battle to Rye   15.3 miles (24.7km)

- **Time** 5hrs 30mins actual walking time   • **Total ascent** 540m/1771ft
- **Map** OS Explorer *124 Hastings & Bexhill; 125 Romney Marsh, Rye & Winchelsea*

The route out of Battle follows the 1066 Country Walk, with its red roundels, over gently undulating Sussex woods and farmland for **5 miles** to Westfield. The way climbs steeply as you approach the top of the downs at Icklesham, reached after **5 miles**, followed by another gentle stretch, with views out to sea, for **2.3 miles** to Winchelsea. After Winchelsea comes a steep descent to the marshes, where you leave the route of the 1066 Country Walk and strike out for **3 miles** to reach Rye.

Rye to Appledore   12.3 miles (19.8km)

- **Time** 4hrs 15mins actual walking time   • **Total ascent** 142m/466ft
- **Map** OS Explorer *125 Romney Marsh, Rye & Winchelsea*

Make sure you have plenty of food and water with you on this section. It's over low-lying, and very flat, Romney Marsh. From Rye you pick up the route of the Saxon Shore Way along the River Rother, and then the Royal Military Canal, before crossing farmland to the first of four lovely Romney Marsh churches, at Fairfield, reached after **5.9 miles.** Brookland is a further **1.9 miles**, followed by Brenzett in **1.8 miles** and Snargate in **1.4 miles**. The railway station at Appledore is another **1.3 miles**.

Day walk options

If you only have one day, start the walk from Rye.

- **By public transport** Railway stations in Battle, Winchelsea, Rye & Appledore.
- **Taxi option** Canterbury Taxis (☎ 01227 444444, 🖳 canterburytaxis.co.uk)

Where to eat or stay along the way

- **Battle** Stay at the *Abbey Hotel* (☎ 01424-772755, 🖳 abbeyhotelbattle.co.uk, 84 High St).

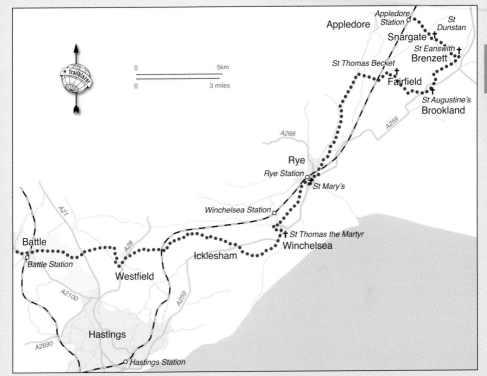

● **Westfield Eat** at the *New Inn* (☎ 01424-752800, 🖳 newinnwestfield.com; food Sat noon-3pm, Main Rd) or later, when you reach **Icklesham**, eat at the *Queen's Head* (☎ 01424-814552, 🖳 queenshead.com; food noon-8pm, to 9pm Fri & Sat).

● **Rye Stay** at *The Standard Inn* (☎ 01797-225231, 🖳 thestandardinnrye.co.uk, The Mint) or *Haydens* (☎ 01797-224501, 🖳 haydensinrye.co.uk, 108 High St). **Drink** at the *Waterworks Micropub* (☎ 01797-224110, 🖳 ryewaterworks.co.uk; noon-10pm, Tower St) and choose from a dozen local ales or ciders. **Eat** at *Webbe's at the Fish Café* (☎ 01797-222210, 🖳 webbesrestaurants.co.uk; 6pm-9.30pm, Tower St) where booking is essential.

● **Snargate Drink** to mark the last leg of your walk at the *Red Lion* (🖳 theromney marsh.net/redlion; noon-4pm, 7pm-10.30pm, a perfect time-warp pub.

PILGRIMAGE HIGHLIGHTS

● **Visit Battle Abbey** (🖳 english-heritage.org.uk; 10am-4pm) where William the Conqueror's victory, church-building and pilgrimage all come together.

● Enjoy a fine variety of landscapes, from woodland walking to **sea views**.

● Explore the pilgrim town of Winchelsea, and its church of **St Thomas** (🖳 winchelseachurch.co.uk; 10am-4pm, German St).

● Climb the tower at **St Mary's**, Rye (🖳 ryeparishchurch.org.uk; 9.15am-5.15pm, winter to 4.15pm, Church Sq) for the spectacular views over Romney Marsh.

Above: Battle Abbey.

Battle

The walk begins in Battle. It may be that Henry II passed through here in 1174 and stopped at the Great Abbey built by William the Conqueror. Henry was on his penitential journey to beg forgiveness for the murder of Thomas Becket, Archbishop of Canterbury and 'turbulent priest'.

1066 Country

The High Weald is a fine stretch of walking country. From the abbey I follow signs for the 1066 Country Walk through Battle Great Wood, 450 acres of deep, dark coniferous woodland and sweet chestnut coppice where badgers and deer lurk, and which enfold the walker like a cosy old cardigan. I emerge, blinking in the light, to navigate Sedlescombe Golf Course. I'm not keen on crossing golf courses. In my experience, golfers and walkers go together about as well as postmen and dogs but this time I am waved cheerily on my way.

Then it's on over fields where the pale stubble hints at winter, towards the undulating ridge that will guide me to Winchelsea via the villages of Westfield and Icklesham.

It is Harvest Supper time, and the churches of St John the Baptist, Westfield and All Saints, Icklesham are being decorated with sheaves of wheat, pumpkins,

jars of preserves and flowers from country gardens. At Icklesham, while the church is being prepared, the organist is practising *We Plough the Fields and Scatter*. It is the perfect hymn for this bright autumn day, and I join in under my breath.

The scramble up to Icklesham has brought a great reward. As I walk on towards the hilltop village of Winchelsea, a calm sea glows a gentle blue to the south, and cargo boats riding at anchor get in a little sunbathing as they wait to round the Straits of Dover for berths at London, Hamburg and elsewhere.

The pilgrim port of Winchelsea

Winchelsea is a 13th century new town and was a major embarkation point for pilgrims headed for Jerusalem and Santiago de Compostela. Two monastic houses – the Franciscans (Greyfriars) and the Dominicans (Blackfriars) – catered for them, and the monastic ruins remain.

2

Above: Windmill near Winchelsea.
Below: Winchelsea – St Thomas's church and (inset) Spike Milligan's gravestone.

New Winchelsea was created, in a piece of very early town planning, as a *bastide* town – the streets laid out in a uniform grid – after the old village down on the levels was devastated in storms. The extensive, vaulted Caen stone cellars under 50 houses were once wine stores, used by merchants who traded with Gascony from what was one of the most important ports in England. That was before the harbour silted up and left Winchelsea land-locked, ending the trade in both wine and pilgrims.

The parish church of St Thomas the Martyr is a remnant of a cathedral-sized building which, along with the religious houses, would have dwarfed the secular town. When the pilgrims no longer came, the town could not afford the upkeep of the church and the tower and transepts were dismantled. Only the walled-off west end of the choir has survived, but this is

still a lovely church. Don't miss the glorious 20th century stained glass by Douglas Strachan, the 14th century tomb where the Pre-Raphelite John Everett Millais painted a sleeping child wrapped in a tunic for *L' Enfant du Regiment*, and the comedian Spike Milligan's grave in the churchyard.

Rye

Across what was once a broad sheltered harbour is Rye, another hill-top town forsaken by the sea. On a sunny day it can look almost Tuscan in the way it clings to its steep rocky outcrop, with the square tower of 900-year-old St Mary's church at the summit of a still largely intact medieval town.

I stroll up pebble-cobbled Mermaid Street to Watchbell Street. Here the Franciscans, hounded out of Winchelsea in the 1530s, returned in 1910 to build the little Italianate church of St Anthony. The rood cross was donated by Radclyffe Hall, one

Above: Houses in Church Square, Rye.
Below: Landgate, Rye.

of many literary figures to make Rye her home. Another, E F Benson, the creator of *Mapp and Lucia*, gave an organ and spectacular stained-glass window to St Mary's, and lived in Lamb House, formerly home to Henry James. With its many inns and restaurants, Rye is the perfect spot to stay the night.

Romney Marsh

From Rye you descend to Romney Marsh, to follow the River Rother inland. For the first mile or two the Rother is tidal, and sandpipers bob along the sleek grey mud above the waterline.

The path switches from the river to the banks of the Royal Military Canal, dug as a defence against Napoleon. I am on the Saxon Shore Way, a long-distance path which follows what was once the coastline before the marsh was drained. I tack across the fields, beneath a great bell-jar sky, towards the first of four Romney Marsh churches. This is a low, flat land, where there is nothing to stop the wind but you.

St Thomas Becket, Fairfield

The last of the blackberries are in the hedgerows, and craneflies tumble across the sheep-shorn turf as I approach St Thomas Becket at Fairfield, standing stark

and alone on Walland Marsh where, since the Black Death did for the village, its flock really is mainly made up of sheep. You collect the key to the church from a hook on the wall at Becket's Barn Farm, a little up the lane. There is something wonderful about being entrusted with the great heavy iron key to such a sacred place.

To my surprise, the key turns easily, and as I stumble inside a sheep tries to follow me. I close the door of this 12th century church and,

in the dark of the porch, shafts of light come through the cracks in the heavy oak door, and the wind hums and howls outside. The hush inside heightens the sense of sanctuary.

This is the most precious of places, with age-bleached oak rafters, butter-yellow plaster, and 18th century, chest-high, white-painted box pews. Peer in and you see the boxes have benches on all four sides, creating a set of cosy, separate little congregations. On the wall is a picture of the

St Thomas Becket, Fairfield

marsh under flood; the church sailing like a ship on the waters.

Why do I call this and the other three churches on today's walk 'perfect'? Maybe we all have our own definition but, for me, it is that Romney Marsh's ancient, remote churches are havens of physical shelter and spiritual sustenance in a harsh environment. It's about the contrast between the starkest of landscapes and the warmth of these places, and the loving care with which their few parishioners tend them.

Above: Bell tower, St Augustine's, Brookland.

MARSH MIRACLE

St Thomas Becket at Fairfield is unusual in that it is the only church in the Canterbury diocese dedicated to this saint, who was archbishop of Canterbury from 1162 until his murder in 1170. Could there be a reason he is particularly venerated here? Local legend offers one. The story goes that a subsequent Archbishop of Canterbury was travelling across Romney Marsh when, at Fairfield, he fell into a ditch and almost drowned. With virtually his last breath he cried out, praying to St Thomas to save him. A shepherd heard his calls and rescued him, and the archbishop had this church built here, dedicating it to the saint.

There is a further Becket connection in St Augustine's, Brookland where, in 1964, a 13th century wall painting depicting Becket's martyrdom was discovered during repairs. The painting, in which Becket kneels in the foreground as one of four murderers thrusts a sword into his skull, had been whitewashed over, presumably at the Reformation.

St Augustine's, Brookland

On I go across the marsh to St Augustine's, Brookland, with its cedar shingle-clad octagonal bell tower standing apart from the church because the marshy land could not support a conventional bell tower. Inside is a heavy lead font dating from 1200, and decorated with two tiers of illustrations, one featuring the signs of the zodiac, the other the months of the agricultural year. It is said to have been stolen by Romney raiders from a church in Normandy, which would explain why March is illustrated with the distinctly non-marsh activity of vine pruning, and October with grape pressing.

St Eanswith's, Brenzett

It is just a short hop along quiet lanes to Brenzett and St Eanswith. Eanswith was

Barham, dubbed Romney Marsh 'the Fifth Continent'. He wrote: 'The world, according to the best geographers, is divided into Europe, Asia, Africa, America and Romney Marsh'. Barham was right: the marsh really is a place apart and, even today, the modern world has not quite managed to obliterate its other-worldly air.

Snargate is also home to the most perfect, time-warp pub: The Red Lion. It dates from the 16th century, has been in the same family for over 100 years, and was last redecorated in 1890.

I certainly find it a welcome haven, as precious in its way as the four wonderful Romney Marsh churches, and the perfect place to rest before tackling the last leg of my pilgrimage: up the road to the country station at Appledore, and the train home.

Above: Memorial in St Eanswith's, Brenzett.

an Anglo-Saxon princess, granddaughter of King Ethelbert of Kent, who was converted to Christianity by St Augustine, the subject of Walk 1. This church has a curious tomb, featuring stone carvings of two moustachioed men lying side by side, the one at the back raising himself up on an elbow as if about to have a chat with the other. They were father and son, both named John Fagge, who died within seven years of each other in the 17th century. Their tomb was the inspiration for Edith Nesbit's ghost story *Man Size in Marble*.

St Dunstan's, Snargate

From Brenzett, I take a winding green road to Snargate and St Dunstan's, where two fat orange pumpkins sit side by side on the bench in the porch. It was here that a demoralised 19th century vicar, Richard

3

Blake, Jerusalem and St Richard

Haslemere to Chichester

Following St Richard's pilgrim path through the
landscape that inspired William Blake
to write *Jerusalem*

In his poem *Jerusalem*, William Blake asks: 'And did those feet, in ancient time, walk upon England's mountains green?' following up with: 'And was the Holy Lamb of God, in England's pleasant pastures seen?'

Those questions were inspired by the scenery on this pilgrimage. Not that Blake found mountains in West Sussex, but he did find the rolling, richly verdant South Downs, and in particular a hill called The Trundle, or St Roche's Hill, which he observed on regular walks to the village of Lavant.

Blake is not the only inspiration for this pilgrimage. On the path to Chichester you also follow in the footsteps of pilgrims who, in the Middle Ages, passed through Midhurst on their way to St Richard's shrine in Chichester Cathedral which, pre-Reformation, was the third most popular place of veneration in England. Today, it is probably fair to say that Richard of Chichester is among the lesser-known saints, but you may well be familiar with the final lines of a prayer he wrote:

May I know thee more clearly, Love thee more dearly,
And follow thee more nearly.'

The lane up to Black Down.

PRACTICAL INFORMATION

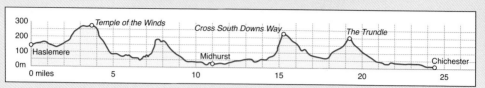

- **Terrain** Sustained ascents and descents on tracks through dense woodland and over grass. May be muddy after rain.
- **Difficulty** Moderate
- **Directions & GPS*** 003.pdf, 003.gpx, 003.kml at ▣ https://trailblazer-guides.com/press

* See p10-11 for more information on downloads

ROUTE OVERVIEW   25.4 miles (40.9km)

Wonderful walking from the wooded Surrey Hills through the rolling South Downs National Park, offering great variety and stunning views. To give you plenty of time to see Chichester cathedral at the end, you could consider breaking the Midhurst to Chichester section at Charlton to make two shorter days.

Haslemere to Midhurst   11.4 miles (18.3km)

- **Time** 4hrs 30mins actual walking time   ● **Total ascent** 714m/2342ft
- **Map** OS Explorer *OL33 Haslemere & Petersfield*

From Haslemere station follow the B2131 for **0.7 mile,** then join the route of the Serpent Trail and continue on paths and tracks up into the National Trust's heavily wooded Black Down. You leave the Serpent Trail on the heights, and reach the Temple of the Winds, the highest point, after **3.2 miles**. Wind down through woods and farmland via Fernhurst for **6.5 miles** to Easebourne. After Easebourne Priory and Cowdray Castle you reach Midhurst **1 mile** beyond.

PILGRIMAGE HIGHLIGHTS

- Enjoy the incredible views from **The Temple of the Winds** and the top of **The Trundle** (St Roche's Hill), among the finest in the South Downs National Park.
- Explore the pilgrim church of **St Margaret of Antioch** at **Fernhurst** (Church Rd, 10am-4pm).
- Visit St Mary's church at the former convent of **Easebourne Priory**, Midhurst.
- On a Sunday catch the church service at 13th century **St James, Heyshott** (▣ heyshott.org.uk, services 1st & 4th Sun of the month: 11.15am, 2nd & 3rd Sun: 9.30am) at the foot of the downs.
- Visit St Richard's tomb at **Chichester Cathedral** and stay for Evensong/Evening Prayer (▣ chichestercathedral.org.uk).

St Richard's feast day: 3 April Catholic church, 16 June Anglican Church.

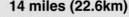

Midhurst to Chichester

14 miles (22.6km)

- **Time** 5hrs 15mins actual walking time
- **Total ascent** 661m/2168ft
- **Map** OS Explorer *OL8 Chichester*

The terrain is easier on this stretch, being mainly beside farmland and through woods via several villages. From Midhurst the New Lipchis Way guides you **7 miles** to Charlton, crossing the South Downs after Heyshott. From Charlton it's an easy climb **1.6 miles** up the lane to the top of The Trundle with views over Goodwood and south to Chichester. Then it's down a chalk lane all the way to pretty Lavant (**2.5 miles**) to pick up the Centurion Way (a disused railway track) for **2.9 miles** into Chichester.

Day walk options

Either section would make a fine one-day walk.

- **By public transport** Railway stations at Haslemere and Chichester; buses from Midhurst to both.
- **Taxi option** Haslemere Taxis (☎ 01428-481464, 🖳 haslemere-taxis.co.uk); Chichester Taxis (☎ 01243-778499, 🖳 chichester-taxis.co.uk).

Where to eat or stay along the way

- **Haslemere Stay** opposite the railway station at the *Station House* (☎ 01428-776560, 🖳 thestation househaslemere.co.uk) a cosy pub-with-rooms.
- **Fernhurst** Have **lunch** at the *Red Lion* (☎ 01428-643112, 🖳 red-lion-fernhurst.co.uk; food Mon-Sat noon-3pm & 6-9pm; Sun noon-4pm).
- **Midhurst** Treat yourself to a **cream tea** at the *Cowdray Farm Shop Café* (☎ 01730-815152, Cowdray Park; daily 9am-5pm. **Stay** at either the *Swan Inn* (☎ 01730-859557, 🖳 swanmidhurst.com, Red Lion St), or the 3-star *Angel Inn* (☎ 01730-812421, 🖳 theangelmidhurst.co.uk, North St). Have a **drink** in the cosy Gin Bar at the **Spread Eagle** Hotel, an ancient coaching inn on South St or go Spanish at **Faustino's Wine and Tapas Bar** (☎ 01730-814745, 🖳 faustinosmidhurst.co.uk; daily from 5pm, North St).
- **Charlton** Eat lunch at historic pub *The Fox Goes Free* (☎ 01243-811461, 🖳 thefoxgoesfree.com; Mon-Fri noon-2.30pm & 6.15-9.30pm, Sat noon-10pm, Sun noon-5pm & 6.15-9.30pm).
- **Chichester** Good selection of places to eat or stay.

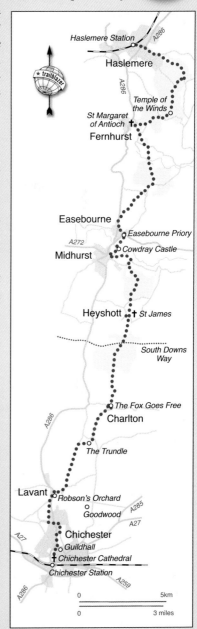

The sun is burning off the early-morning mist from Black Down as I follow the sunken lane up this great, wooded ridge from Haslemere. The bracken is steaming, and sweet chestnuts are parachuting to the ground, shrugging off their acid-green jackets as they land.

Last night's rain has brought the woods out in a rash of fungi. Tiny pale mushrooms poke wet from the vivid moss on a decaying log. Alarm-bell-red fly agaric toadstools form a fairy ring beside my path as I wind my way south along the ridge.

The Temple of the Winds

To gaze out from the grandstand of The Temple of the Winds is to experience a transformation. Named after a Bronze Age circular bank, this is the highest point in the South Downs National Park, with views sweeping way to the south. This is a place to make you feel small, both in space and in time.

As I look out, the last wisps of morning mist are vanishing from an ice-blue sky, in which the only modern intrusion is a few feeble silver darts of planes rising from Gatwick.

St Margaret's, Fernhurst

Winding south-west down to the village of Fernhurst might feel like an anti-climax, if it weren't for this 11th century pilgrim church. As the church guide notes, St Margaret of Antioch was 'perhaps

built by a soldier of the Cross in gratitude for his safe return from the crusades,' St Margaret being the crusaders' favourite saint. The welcome on the church door invites you to 'Stay a while and be still – let go your burden and share the serenity of this place'.

From here I pick up a green highway in the woods. This ancient drove road runs wide and die-straight through the forested Low Weald, still bounded by the moss-cloaked, tree-sprouting remnants of ragstone walls.

Easebourne Priory

At Easebourne, the Grade I-listed stone country house you look on today began life as Easebourne Priory, in 1248. St Mary's church, which is attached to it, housed the chapel of the Prioress and 10 Benedictine nuns who lived at the priory.

The central section of this building was the chapter house, where the community

gathered. On the first floor was the Dorter, or sleeping quarters, probably divided into cells for the nuns, and behind it is the cloister. To the left is the nuns' refectory.

Margaret Cary writes, in *Easebourne Priory and Church*, that during an inspection in 1414 'the Prioress was ordered to sell her trimmings of costly fur and her jewels, and exception was taken to the lapdogs and pet monkeys with which the ladies beguiled their leisure hours.' In 1535, at the Reformation, the nuns were thrown out and their property confiscated. The church roof was torn off and the building left open to the elements for 300 years. Henry VIII gave the priory to Sir William Fitzwilliam, owner of Cowdray House just to the south.

Above: Following the old drove road south of Fernhurst.
Left: The view from The Temple of the Winds, Black Down. You can see as far as the South Downs, which you will cross south of Heyshott.

3

Cowdray and Guy Fawkes

Cowdray was one of England's great Tudor houses, comparable to the finest palaces, and Henry VIII visited three times during his reign. The house was largely destroyed by fire in 1793, but the surviving ruins are impressive enough to have received Grade I listing. A curse was said to have been put on the house by a monk ejected from Battle Abbey, which Henry gave to Anthony Browne, Fitzwilliam's half-brother and heir. In 1592 the 2nd Viscount Anthony-Maria Browne employed Guy Fawkes as a footman, and was imprisoned for complicity in the Gunpowder Plot, after having been warned to stay away from Parliament on 5 November 1605.

In 1591 Elizabeth I was entertained here for five days. Anthony Browne, 1st Viscount Montague of Cowdray, was Catholic, but retained royal favour, and a banquet was held for the queen in the refectory. As part of the entertainment, an actor playing the part of a pilgrim – despite pilgrimage having been outlawed by her father – led Elizabeth to an oak tree where the heraldry of the county was displayed, and a 'green man', dressed in ivy, expressed Cowdray's loyalty to her.

Midhurst

Midhurst is at an ancient pilgrim crossroads. From the 1200s, the paths of pilgrims making for St Swithin's shrine in Winchester, and those headed for the shrine of St Richard at the new cathedral in Chichester, crossed here. To cater for them the Knights Hospitaller, who were responsible for the welfare of pilgrims, built a chapel to St Thomas Becket, and a pilgrim hostelry, in West Street. The Hospitallers' assets were seized by Henry VIII in 1540, and later demolished.

St James, Heyshott

Chichester pilgrims might also have paused at the foot of the Downs in Heyshott, at the 13th century church of St James. Pinned to the church door is a prayer that reminds you every pilgrim also needs a place of belonging, asking: 'O God, whose son was content to share the life of his village at Nazareth: Bless, we beseech

BLAKE, *JERUSALEM* AND THE WOMEN'S INSTITUTE

Blake's title for the poem that has become known as *Jerusalem* was *And Did Those Feet In Ancient Time*. In it he reflects upon the myth that Jesus Christ might have visited England with Joseph of Arimathea, his tin-dealer uncle, walking over landscapes such as the 'green and pleasant land' of Sussex, establishing here a heaven on earth: a new Jerusalem. A century after it was written, poet laureate Robert Bridges included it in an anthology of patriotic verse collated in response to the horrifying casualty count at the Battle of the Somme. Hubert Parry set the words to music and, renamed *Jerusalem*, it became one of the best-loved English hymns. It was adopted by the women's suffrage movement and then by the Women's Institute, whose anthem it still is. In a piece of perfect synchronicity, the very first WI was founded in the village of Charlton, in The Fox Goes Free pub which is also on our route.

Opposite: The ruins of Cowdray House, once a grand Tudor mansion.

thee, the life of this village with thy continual presence.'

From here, if you walk this way from July through to February, you will likely find the rising plain of woods and fields alive with pheasants. They panic noisily, all except one brave creature that appoints itself my pilgrim guide, strutting along at my heels before scurrying ahead to look back and encourage me onward and upward.

The Fox Goes Free, Charlton

The next village, Charlton, plays a significant part in the story of Blake's *Jerusalem*. At The Fox Goes Free – the name referring to the point in its history when the pub became a free house – a plaque in the back bar reads: 'On 9 November 1915 the first Womans [sic] Institute meeting in England was held in this room.' The organisation adopted the hymn as its anthem in 1924.

The Trundle, St Roche's Hill

Cresting the downs, you reach the summit of The Trundle, which has been a sacred gathering place for 5000 years. This is the heart of William Blake country. It was the view of this place from Lavant to the south that inspired Blake to write the poem which became *Jerusalem*. In the 14th century there was a pilgrim chapel here, dedicated to St Roche. Born in Montpellier around 1350, St Roche survived the Black Death, and his chapel was visited by the sick who considered it a place of healing. The chapel building was destroyed in the Reformation but its oval footprint has since been revealed by archaeological investigation.

The Trundle offers a view to match that from The Temple of the Winds, with the villages of East and Mid Lavant pointing the way to Chichester, where the slender cathedral spire makes a particularly elegant finishing post.

Below: Perfect views from The Trundle: east over Goodwood racetrack and south to Chichester

3

Above, left: Robson's Orchard. **Right**: The Centurion Way, a disused railway line, to Chichester.

Lavant and Robson's Orchard

In the early 1800s Blake visited Robson's Orchard in Lavant every Tuesday and Friday to 'take a dish of coffee' with his friend, a wealthy spinster called Harriet Poole, who lived here. He called her the Lady of Lavant. You will find Robson's Orchard tucked in on the left, just after the Earl of March pub, although as it's a private house it can only be viewed from the road. At the time, Blake was a jobbing en-

graver who hoped to make a living as a miniaturist. He was introduced to Miss Poole as a possible client while doing some work for a painter and poet called William Hayley. Hayley lived in Felpham, near Bognor Regis, and Blake took a cottage there for three years.

Chichester Guildhall

The track of a disused railway, now a cycle path known as the Centurion Way, takes

Below: On the chalk road south of The Trundle

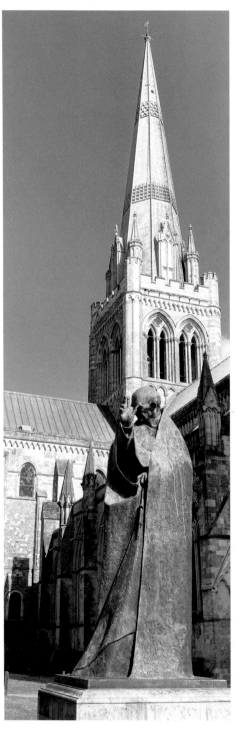

me to Chichester, where the Guildhall forms another significant William Blake landmark. It was here, in 1804, that he was tried and acquitted of the capital offences of treason and sedition.

In a curious episode, Blake had been confronted by a drunken soldier, John Schofield, who he discovered in his garden in Felpham. Blake was accused of assaulting Schofield, who claimed Blake said 'Damn the King ... damn his soldier, they are all slaves.' Blake wrote *And Did Those Feet* while awaiting trial, and later depicted Schofield wearing 'mind-forged manacles' in an illustration to the poem.

Chichester Cathedral

St Richard of Chichester, patron saint of Sussex, stands on a plinth on the approach to his cathedral, raising his hand as if beckoning the pilgrim on.

Richard was as big a rebel in his way as free-thinking, anti-authoritarian Blake: a teetotal vegetarian who wore a hair shirt, refused to eat off silver, fought against clerical corruption and supported papal rights against the king. Richard's tomb became a place of pilgrimage, rivalling that of Thomas Becket at Canterbury in popularity. His tomb was destroyed at the Reformation but re-established in 1930, in the retro-quire beyond the high altar.

A relic, part of Richard's forearm, is buried beneath the St Richard Altar, which stands flanked by a statue and icon of the saint. Here, pilgrims can collect a card bearing Richard's prayer, which he is said to have recited on his deathbed:

Left: The bronze statue of St Richard by Philip Jackson stands outside Chichester Cathedral and was dedicated in 2000. St Richard's right hand is raised in blessing; in his left he holds a scourge, a symbol of self sacrifice.

'Thanks be to Thee, my Lord Jesus Christ
For all the benefits Thou hast given me,
For all the pains and insults Thou hast borne for me.
O most merciful Redeemer, friend and brother,
May I know Thee more clearly,
Love Thee more dearly,
And follow Thee more nearly.'

And maybe you might echo Blake, whose deep if unorthodox spiritual yearning led him to vow:
'I will not cease from mental fight,
Nor shall my sword sleep in my hand:
Till we have built Jerusalem,
In England's green and pleasant land.'

Left: Stained glass window by Marc Chagall, unveiled in Chichester Cathedral in 1978. It is a visual interpretation of Psalm 150: 'Let everything that hath breath praise the Lord'. The artist was 88 when he created this work.
Below: St Richard's shrine and icon of the saint.

4

A prehistoric pilgrimage
Avebury to Stonehenge, Wiltshire

A pre-Christian pilgrimage through the Avebury and Stonehenge World Heritage Sites via an ancient ceremonial route along the valley of the River Avon

I met a shaman at Avebury stone circle. A shaman called Siobhan. She cut a striking figure in her cloak, fur hat, pelts and flowing blonde locks. I told her I was on my way to Stonehenge, and she told me why she preferred Avebury.

'Stonehenge is all about life and death,' she said, 'and mostly death. Avebury is about healing.'

Well, certainly, one theory is that to travel to Stonehenge along the River Avon symbolised a ritual passage from life to death: a journey in celebration of ancestors and the recently deceased. I was about to depart on that journey but, before I did, I asked Siobhan more about Avebury as a sort of Neolithic Lourdes. She handed me her coppiced hazel staff, with its goat's head handle, and tried to help me feel Avebury's healing power. I held the staff with both hands, the head facing away from me. I felt a buzz pass from the staff into my hands. I turned the goat's head to face me, then to the right, then the left. Siobhan told me to think of the words 'down' or 'sink'. Then the word 'rise'.

What did I feel? Well, there were certainly vibrations. Rooted in the rational, I wondered aloud whether the trucks grinding past on the A4361, which dog-legs through the sacred circle, carving Avebury into a yin and yang, could have anything to do with what I felt?

'No, that's not it at all,' said Siobhan. 'Some people hold the staff and get flung over backwards.' These seemed to be people who had suffered post-traumatic stress. One had fought in Afghanistan.

Despite the road, Avebury is still incredibly impressive. I walked twice around the stones on the towering, encircling rampart, soaking in the mystery. On Christian pilgrimages you know why the places are there and what they mean. Here you can't be sure. Was this a place of ritual, a sacred space in which to fulfil a spiritual need? If so, creating Avebury and Stonehenge came from the same impetus as building great churches. Certainly, walking here, it is easy to feel an affinity with those who built it. Like us, they were investing their faith in a mystery.

Avebury Stone Circle

PRACTICAL INFORMATION

- **Terrain** Sustained and sometimes steep ascents and descents, mainly on grass paths and rough tracks. Can be muddy in places. Short stretches on generally quiet lanes.
- **Difficulty** Challenging
- **Directions & GPS*** 004.pdf, 004.gpx, 004.kml at 🖳 https://trailblazer-guides.com/press

* See p10-11 for more information on downloads

ROUTE OVERVIEW   26.9 miles (43.3km)

A walk of big skies and mystical landscapes, punctuated by pretty little villages. Make sure you're equipped for all weathers and check the forecast before you set off as Salisbury Plain is very exposed with little or no shelter from sun or rain.

Avebury to Upavon   13.4 miles (21.6km)

- **Time** 5hrs 30mins actual walking time   ● **Total ascent** 401m/1320ft
- **Map** OS Explorer *157 Marlborough & Savernake Forest; 130 Salisbury & Stonehenge*

Soon after Avebury you pick up the Ridgeway national trail for a short distance, well signposted with an acorn symbol. You reach East Kennet after **2.6 miles** before heading to Adam's Grave, a Neolithic burial mound, reached in **2.7 miles**, then descending to Alton Barnes **(1.4 miles)** and Honeystreet **(0.4 miles)**. From here the route follows the White Horse Trail beside the Kennet and Avon Canal, leaving it for Woodborough **(1.5 miles)** along a mix of lanes, tracks and footpaths via Bottlesford **(0.7 miles)** and Charlton St Peter **(2.4 miles)** to reach Upavon after **1.7 miles**.

PILGRIMAGE HIGHLIGHTS

- **Avebury Stone Circle** (🖳 english-heritage.org.uk/visit/places/avebury/ SN8 1RF).
- Climb to the summit of **Adam's Grave**, a Neolithic long barrow.
- Follow the valley of the River Avon through a string of peaceful villages, and have a picnic on the riverbank.
- Explore **Woodhenge** (🖳 english-heritage.org.uk/visit/places/woodhenge/) before your final approach along the ceremonial Avenue to the climax: **Stonehenge** (🖳 english-heritage.org.uk/visit/places/stonehenge/; 9.30am-5pm winter, to 8pm summer; entry by timed ticket, must be booked in advance). To make your way home, catch the Stonehenge Tour bus (🖳 thestonehengetour.info, last bus 4pm winter, 7pm summer) to Salisbury railway station.

Upavon to Stonehenge

13.5 miles (21.7km)

- **Time** 5hrs 30mins actual walking time
- **Total ascent** 525m/1425ft
- **Map** OS Explorer *130 Salisbury & Stonehenge*

Climb from Upavon to the fringes of Salisbury Plain and skirt it before a long gentle descent to the Avon Valley, and a string of riverside villages, reaching Enford in **4.5 miles**, Combe in **0.9 miles**, Netheravon in **1.4 miles** before climbing gently to reach Woodhenge in **4.3 miles** and Stonehenge in **2.4 miles**.

Day walk options

Either leg of this route would make a good one-day walk.

- **By public transport** To reach Avebury stone circle take the train to Swindon and a bus or taxi from there to Avebury. Upavon is accessible by bus or taxi from Swindon or Salisbury. There is a regular shuttle bus from Stonehenge to the railway station at Salisbury.
- **Taxi option** 24/7 Swindon Taxis (☎ 01793-469247, 🖥 247swindontaxis.co.uk)

Where to eat or stay along the way

- **Swindon** Stay at the *Great Western Hotel*, Swindon (☎ 01793-694997, 🖥 thegwhotelswindon.co.uk, 73 Station Rd) opposite the railway station, then take a **bus** or **taxi** to Avebury the next morning.
- **Honeystreet** Have **lunch** beside the Kennet and Avon Canal at either *The Barge* pub (☎ 01672-851222, 🖥 thebargeinnhoneystreet.co.uk; Mon-Sat noon-3pm & 5.30-8pm; Sun noon-4.30pm), or the *Honeystreet Mill Café* (☎ 01672-851853, 🖥 honeystreetmillcafe.co.uk; Mon-Sat 9am-5pm, Sun 10am-5pm).
- **Upavon** Stay at **The Antelope**, a lovely village inn (☎ 01980-630025, 🖥 antelopeupavon.co.uk, 3 High St). Before you set off the next day buy your packed lunch ingredients from **Londis** on the High St, for a picnic on the riverbank.

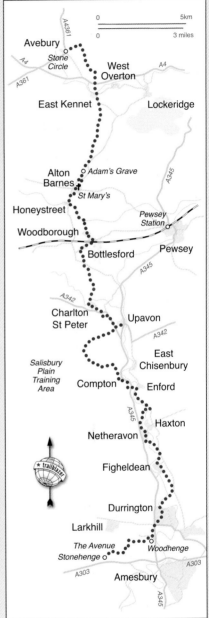

AVEBURY STONE CIRCLE

Avebury stone circle is a Neolithic – later Stone Age – henge monument comprising three stone circles enclosed with a ditch and bank. The outer stones form the largest megalithic stone circle in the world: 350m in diameter, 1000m in circumference. Avebury was built over several hundred years in the third millennium BC and, although its purpose cannot be confirmed, it is believed to have been used in ritual or ceremony.

From the 14th to 18th centuries, residents of the village which had grown within the circle destroyed many of the stones. Some were broken up as building material, others toppled and buried for religious reasons, since the monument had become associated with the devil. In the 20th century the site was investigated by archaeologists, and many buried stones were righted. The skeleton of a man was found crushed beneath a 10ft (3m) high stone in the hole that had been dug to receive it.

Avebury may have been part of a geographically wider ritual complex containing many monuments with differing religious and celebratory functions.

Most pilgrimages benefit enormously from good weather. To me, this one is different. It suits more dramatic conditions. The sky glowered down at me as I walked up Overton Hill to join the Ridgeway, the ancient path along the top of the Marlborough Downs. This is a landscape on which ancient man made his mark – many marks – over millennia. There are many enclosures, long-barrow burial chambers, and tumuli.

4

Avebury Sanctuary

Adam's Grave

Passing East Kennet I keep climbing, across downland given a close clipper-cut from the sheep which, wisely this morning, are hunkered down in a hollow scooped out of the hillside by centuries of wind. As I look down into the valley, I see black calves gathered in a barn, and suddenly the day brightens. But it's the acid light of a day whose mood can easily change, and at a peak called Adam's Grave it does. The wind hits me, hard, from the north east, almost toppling me over as I stand at the summit of this long-barrow on a hill.

Maybe Adam doesn't like me standing on him. Excavations here found partial human skeletons in a chamber lined with sarsen stones. I brace myself against the wind and scan hillsides etched with serpentine ramparts and ditches: abstract designs in the turf, like a giant's doodles.

On the way down towards the Vale of Pewsey I look back and see the White Horse of Alton Barnes cut bright white

Below: View from the summit of Adam's Grave.

Above: White Horse at Alton Barnes.

Above: Kennet & Avon Canal, Honeystreet.

into the chalk. Suddenly things get a good deal more civilised. This is gentle English countryside: silent villages; verges bright with snowdrops; Saxon churches like St Mary's, half hidden in its leafy churchyard at Alton Barnes; ponies in fields; and, somehow incongruously, the Kennet and Avon canal at Honeystreet.

Honeystreet to Upavon
The Honeystreet Mill Café and the Barge pub make this a perfect lunch stop. The canal feels like something of an anomaly up here in the heart of the downs, but it was once a vital transport artery, linking Bristol and the Avon with Reading and the Thames. Dug between 1794 and 1810, it was superseded by the Great Western Railway, fell into disrepair but was restored by enthusiasts, and now offers a pleasant contrast to the landlocked route I have followed so far.

Once I have manoeuvred gingerly past a highly territorial swan I take its towpath

Above: Woodborough Hill from the canal.
Below: Woodhenge circle.

for a mile or so, before heading off to Woodborough, the first of a series of pleasant villages that line the paths, tracks and quiet lanes to Upavon. Bottlesford follows, with the Seven Stars pub and a phone box enterprisingly recycled into a tourist information point. Then comes the gentle descent via Charlton St Peter to Upavon, the half-way point and suggested overnight stop, with its two pubs and village shop.

**DANGER
IMPACT AREA
KEEP OUT**

early morning lift off, and riffing through the 300 syllables of their uplifting song, raise my spirits. You could stay on the plain, skirting the sign-marked danger area, and head straight for Stonehenge. That would be quicker, but a far lesser walk, especially if you are accompanied by the sounds of the Army wargaming in the restricted zone to the west.

Much better to head down towards Compton in the valley, to follow the silver ribbon of the River Avon. This is a truly fine stretch of walking country, and a refreshing contrast to yesterday's downland. The path follows the river fairly closely and there are numerous potential picnic spots along the way. The route, and the river, thread their way through a string of villages including East Chisenbury and Enford, with its thatched pub, The Swan. Each village has at least one former water mill and, in Netheravon, theirs has been put to perfect use as the Stonehenge Ales brewery.

Salisbury Plain to the River Avon valley

The next day begins with a sustained climb up onto Salisbury Plain. This can seem a little too like a blasted heath with its army posts, warning signs of unexploded bombs and tracks churned up by tanks. But the skylarks, achieving

The ancient ceremonial route

A climb out of a brief belt of suburbia at Durrington brings you to Woodhenge, a site contemporary with Stonehenge but which was only discovered in 1926, and where stumpy concrete pillars mark the positions of the original timber post-holes. It might be tempting to hurry on, given what is in store a little over 2 miles (3km) away. But once you learn that excavations at the centre of the Woodhenge circle uncovered the grave of a child, its skull split in sacrifice, you realise this strange place warrants a little time and contemplation.

Then comes the final walk along the course of The Avenue, the original ceremonial approach which led from the River Avon to Stonehenge. The last stretch is aligned with the summer solstice sunrise, which suggests that was the most significant time to come here.

The stones appear as a pile of collapsed Jenga on the horizon, gradually revealing themselves through a long approach that is like walking up the nave of a vast open-air cathedral. This is the route Stonehenge pilgrims took for millennia, and it is by far the best route to take today. You avoid the traffic-jammed A303 and the vast bulk of visitors, who are herded in via the visitors' centre 1.5 miles to the west of the stones.

The English Heritage staff are quite surprised, and a little curious, to meet a pilgrim who has come all the way from Avebury. I cadge a ride on the shuttle to the visitors' centre.

STONEHENGE

Stonehenge's crowning glory is a ring of 13ft (4m) tall, 25 ton standing stones, with a ring of lintels on top, erected between 3000 and 2000BC, and set in a landscape littered with hundreds of Neolithic and Bronze Age burial mounds and other monuments. It evolved in several phases over 1500 years, with the main stone circle dating from about 2500BC. It uses two types of stone: sarsens from up to 25 miles (40km) away; and blue stones believed to have been brought 150 miles (240km) from the Preseli Hills in Pembrokeshire, west Wales.

Its alignment with sunrise at the summer solstice in June, and sunset at the winter solstice in December, suggests a ritual or religious association. Theories explaining Stonehenge's function range from it being a religious site – it has what is believed to be an altar stone at its centre – to a place of healing, and for ancestor worship. It may have fulfilled several of these functions.

Whatever religious, mystical or spiritual elements were central to Stonehenge, its design includes a celestial observatory function, which might have allowed prediction of eclipse, solstice, equinox and other celestial events important to a contemporary religion. Stonehenge was certainly a burial site, with isotope analysis of discovered remains showing that individuals came from Germany, France and the Mediterranean region, and suggesting that the monument had profound significance for many peoples over a wide area. **Overleaf**: Inside the Stone Circle.

5

Jurassic Coast pilgrimage

Abbotsbury, Chideock, Whitchurch Canonicorum and Lyme Regis

Walking this spectacular coastline from the lonely hilltop chapel of St Catherine, patron saint of single women, via the Catholic martyrs' church at Chideock and the ancient shrine of St Wite at Whitchurch Canonicorum, to Lyme Regis

The Jurassic Coast is so spectacular that simply to walk it feels like a pilgrimage in itself. What could possibly enhance such a landscape? Well, nothing, I would have said, until I looked up from Abbotsbury at the great honeyed-stone, 14th century chapel of St Catherine, standing stark on the summit of a bare hill 80m above Chesil Beach.

The sight made me realise that the Jurassic Coast is also a landscape of faith. Three diverse points of veneration elevate this walk. First comes St Catherine, patron saint of single women; then Chideock with its church dedicated to seven village martyrs who died for their Catholic faith; finally St Wite, an obscure saint whose shrine is, in historic significance, second only to that of Edward the Confessor at Westminster Abbey.

St Catherine's Chapel

PRACTICAL INFORMATION

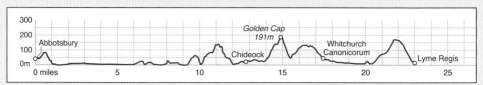

- **Terrain** Mainly shingle beach and cliff paths on Abbotsbury to Chideock section, a mix of footpaths and pavements on Chideock to Lyme Regis section.
- **Difficulty** Mainly moderate, but with some challenging stretches
- **Directions & GPS*** 005.pdf, 005.gpx, 005.kml at 🖳 https://trailblazer-guides.com/press

* See p10-11 for more information on downloads

ROUTE OVERVIEW   22.9 miles (36.9km)

This walk is a switchback ride involving fabulous views from high points as well as beach walking at sea level so allow yourself plenty of rest breaks. Take a packed lunch for the Chideock to Lyme Regis section.

Abbotsbury to Chideock   12.9 miles (20.8km)
- **Time** 5hrs 15mins actual walking time   • **Total ascent** 649m/2130ft
- **Map** OS Explorer *OL15 Purbeck & South Dorset*,

A steep climb out of Abbotsbury to St Catherine's Chapel (**0.6 miles**) is followed by a sharp descent, joining the combined South West Coast Path and Macmillan Way to walk along the flat beach via West Bexington (**3.3 miles**) to Hive Beach (**2.9 miles**). Here the route leaves the coast path briefly, re-joining it at Burton Freshwater (**1 mile**) and climbing over East Cliff to reach West Bay, in **1.3 miles**. A rollercoaster cliff-top ride to Seatown (**3 miles**) follows, where you head inland for Chideock (**0.8 miles**).

Chideock to Lyme Regis   10 miles (16.1km)
- **Time** 4 hours actual walking time   • **Total ascent** 1243m/4080ft
- **Map** OS Explorer *116 Lyme Regis & Bridport*

From Chideock, lanes then tracks reach the coastal summit of Golden Cap (**2 miles**), then you descend and turn inland along farm tracks for the village of Morcomblake (**1.7 miles**), and on quiet lanes to Whitchurch Canonicorum (**1 mile**). A path alongside the River Char takes you to Charmouth (**2.9 miles**) where you re-join the coastal path as it climbs steadily along the main road through the town, then descends steeply to Lyme Regis, reached in **2.4 miles**.

Day walk options
If you only have one day, start from Chideock.
- **By public transport** The nearest railway station to Abbotsbury is Weymouth, and for Lyme Regis it's Axminster. To reach Chideock take a bus or taxi from Axminster.
- **Taxi option** Axminster Taxis (☎ 01297 34000, 🖳 axminster-taxis.co.uk).

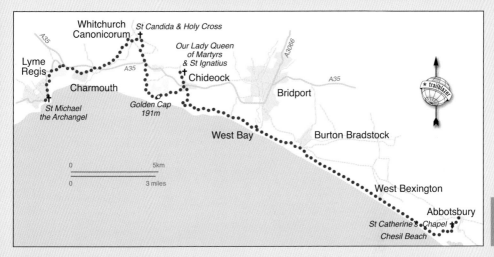

Where to eat or stay along the way

● **Abbotsbury Stay** at the *Ilchester Arms Hotel* (☎ 01305-873841, 🖥 theilchester.co.uk, 9 Market St), or at the *Abbey House* (☎ 01305-871330, 🖥 theabbeyhouse.co.uk, Church St) among the abbey ruins.

● **Hive Beach Lunch** by the sea at *Hive Beach Café* (☎ 01308-897070, 🖥 hivebeachcafe .co.uk, Beach Road; daily from 10am) with crab and lobster from West Bay fishermen.

● **Chideock Stay** at *Chideock House B&B* (☎ 01297-489242, 🖥 chideockhouse.co.uk, Main St) and **eat** at either the *Clock House Inn* (☎ 01297-489423, 🖥 clockchideock .co.uk; food noon-2.30pm & 6-9pm) or the pretty thatched *George Inn* (☎ 01297-489419, 🖥 george innchideock.co.uk; food Thur-Sat & Mon noon-9pm, Tue & Wed 5-9pm, Sun noon-4pm).

● **Whitchurch Canonicorum** The *Five Bells* (☎ 01297-489262, 🖥 thefivebellsinn.pub) currently serves lunch only on a Sunday.

● **Lyme Regis** This seaside town has many options for both staying and eating.

PILGRIMAGE HIGHLIGHTS

● Climb to **St Catherine's Chapel** and enjoy your first view of **Chesil Beach.**

● Visit the hidden **Martyrs Church** chapel (🖥 chideockmartyrschurch.org.uk, church and museum; 10am-4pm) in **Chideock,** which commemorates seven Catholics executed for celebrating mass in the secret barn chapel (contact them in advance to visit the secret part).

● Climb to **Golden Cap,** the highest point of the **Jurassic Coast**, with views east to Portland Bill and west to Start Bay.

● Seek out the shrine to obscure local saint **St Wite,** a place of veneration for a millennium, at **St Candida and Holy Cross, Whitchurch Canonicorum** (🖥 cath edralofthevale.co.uk; 10am-4pm; Services Sun 11am, except first Sun in month 8am)

St Catherine's feast day: 24 or 25 November   *St Wite's feast day: 1 June*

5

On the cliffs approaching West Bay

St Catherine's Chapel, Abbotsbury

From a distance, St Catherine's Chapel looks fragile. Up close, it is monumental: a great solid statement of faith in stone, built in the 14th century from the local golden buff limestone by Benedictine monks of the ruined St Peter's Abbey at Abbotsbury, in the valley below.

St Peter's was destroyed at the Reformation, but St Catherine's – built as a place of pilgrimage and retreat – survived intact, probably because of its later adaptation as a lighthouse, a beacon burning at the top of its turret. Stepping inside I expect the interior to be as intact as the exterior. In fact, it has been stripped back to the bare stone walls, although the ornate barrel-vaulted ceiling survives.

Up until the late 19th century, women from Abbotsbury and visiting pilgrims who sought a husband would leave notes, or petitions, in nooks in the stone known as wishing holes. There is one tucked into a hollow when I visit. Of

Top: St Catherine's from the former abbey.
Above: The chapel's vaulted ceiling.

ST CATHERINE

St Catherine of Alexandria was a 4th century Greek Christian, martyred for being too smart. Her initial crime was that she defied an order from Alexandria's Roman rulers to attend a pagan ritual sacrifice, and persuaded others to join her boycott. When she accused the emperor of persecution, he drafted in 50 philosophers to debate the virtues of Christianity over paganism with her.

Catherine won the debate and, the story goes, so impressed the emperor that he wanted to marry her. She refused, so was tortured on a revolving wheel onto which knives were mounted – giving us the Catherine Wheel firework. When that didn't kill her, and she was decapitated, milk flowed in place of blood. Her status as the patron saint of single women is based partly on that outflow of nurturing milk, partly on the legend that she became a sort of post-mortem bride of Christ.

In the year 800 her relics were taken to the Greek Orthodox monastery at Mount Sinai – where God handed Moses the Ten Commandments – drawing so many pilgrims that it became the richest monastery in the world. Then came her fall: Catherine was removed from the Catholic Church's Universal Calendar of Saints in 1969 on the grounds that she may never have existed. Well, if you're going to set the bar that high...

course, I don't disturb it but I can see it starts with thanks, so maybe a prayer has been answered.

Here, pilgrims would recite St Catherine's prayer, which runs:

A husband, St Catherine,
A handsome one, St Catherine,
A rich one, St Catherine,
A nice one, St Catherine,
And soon, St Catherine.

The singer PJ Harvey, who is from Abbotsbury, incorporated Catherine's prayer into a song called *The Wind*, but inverted it to relate to Catherine herself.

The chapel has never been excavated, but it may be on the site of a pre-Christian temple dedicated to a pagan moon goddess, or to Astarte or Aphrodite, the Queen of the Sky. It is certainly up in the clouds when I visit. As I descend to Chesil Beach, the building dissolves behind me in the sea mist.

Chesil Beach

By the time I reach Chesil Beach the sun has broken through and warms my back as I scrunch along the shingle crest, my steps keeping time with the waves breaking on the shore. The scent of wild garlic fills the air, and the purple seakale is just beginning to unfurl its leaves above the gravel. I snatch a piece and chew: a free, ready-salted pilgrim snack.

It's not exactly spring, but a day that makes you believe spring is at least possible. By lunch it is almost balmy as I take a break at Hive Beach, but then the sandstone cliffs begin and the day goes bipolar: balmy in the dips, vicious on the heights, where the wind is still capable of slapping you in the face. A few times, when I lift my foot, the wind puts it down again in a spot of its own choosing.

The scramble down to West Bay brings you to a fishing village, where sturdy sea walls defeat the breakers trying to gate-

crash the harbour, in which the crab and lobster boats rock at anchor. At St John's church the welcome to pilgrims reads: 'May the way be smooth, may the wind be always at your back, may the sun shine warm upon your face. May God hold you in the palm of his hand.'

Chideock Martyrs Church

After West Bay the scenery changes dramatically: here begins a roller-coaster ride over West Cliff and Doghouse Hill to Seatown, where I head inland to the village of Chideock, my suggestion for an overnight stop.

Here, tucked away up a lane is a Catholic church dedicated to seven men who died for their faith. This Romanesque, weathered-stone church – Our Lady Queen of Martyrs and St Ignatius – has been a place of Catholic refuge since the Reformation, yet looks as if it has been plucked from the Italian countryside.

Mass was celebrated in secret on this spot throughout the centuries when Catholicism was outlawed. The lords of the manor made it a refuge for Catholic priests

Left: West Bay. **Above**: The shrine to the seven Chideock Martyrs.

smuggled in from the continent via Lyme Regis, and for villagers. The present church is 19th century, but through the sacristy is a staircase leading up to the barn loft in which those secret services were held.

Here, the Chideock Martyrs – three chaplains and four villagers executed between 1587 and 1642 – are memorialised. You will need to apply in advance to see this remarkable place, but the church and adjacent museum are open to all.

Golden Cap

The ancient trackway of Pettycrate Lane leads from Chideock to the foot of Golden Cap, the highest cliff on the Jurassic Coast, which towers above you majestically. Then it's a scramble up to the top with views from Portland Bill in the east to Devon's Start Bay in the west, followed by a descent inland, passing the ruins of St Gabriel's chapel. It stands isolated in a field where there was once a hamlet, Stanton St Gabriel.

The story is that in the 12th century, a newly-married couple were shipwrecked in a storm and spent three days drifting in a dinghy. They prayed to St Gabriel and promised, if he saved them, to build a shrine to him wherever they landed. The bride died in her husband's arms as he brought her ashore at the foot of Golden Cap, but the village adopted the saint, and this chapel was established.

Below: Looking east from Golden Cap.

Above: The ruins of St Gabriel's chapel.

St Wite's Well

A mile before the village of More-comblake I look out for St Wite's Well, which was once a significant pilgrim point, but is now reduced to what looks like a butler sink buried in a pasture, fed by an algae-infested pipe and fenced off beside the path. A grey National Trust plaque points out that it is actually more than it seems. Until the 1930s the waters here were believed to offer a cure for eye infections, and periwinkle that grows locally is known as St Candida's Eyes; Candida being another name for Wite.

St Wite and Whitchurch Canonicorum

Of all the countless shrines in England's churches and cathedrals before the Reformation, only two have survived to offer unbroken veneration for pilgrims. One is Edward the Confessor's tomb at Westminster Abbey, which features in Walk 10, the other – remarkably – is in the village church of St Candida and Holy Cross at Whitchurch Canonicorum, which you reach down quiet lanes from Morecomblake.

The shrine, still a very popular place of pilgrimage today, is a curious sight. On the 13th century base is a 14th century Purbeck marble coffin with three large oval openings cut into the side. Into these, known as limb holes, pilgrims once placed their afflicted body parts and prayed for a cure. Today, they have become sort of pigeonholes to the obscure local saint St Wite, also known as St Candida, and are stuffed with petitions bearing prayers for recovery. The original shrine to St Thomas Becket at Canterbury, featured in Walk 1, probably looked like this.

WHO WAS ST WITE?

There are several theories as to the identity of St Wite, or St Candida. One is that her relics were brought here in the 10th century by refugees from Brittany escaping invading Norsemen, and that she was a princess known to the Bretons as Blanche and the Celts as Gwen. Both names also mean white.

A strong local counter-tradition is that St Wite was a Saxon hermit or holy woman martyred by Danish raiders who attacked Charmouth in the 9th century. The story, recounted in the 1732 book *Survey of Dorsetshire* says: 'Whitechurch... took its name from one St Wite a virgin martyr, whose well the inhabitants will shewe you not farre off in the side of an hill, where she lived in prayer and contemplation, unto whose honour a church being built was from her named Whitechurch.'

Whatever the truth, St Wite was clearly remembered as a helper of the sick, and her shrine was a place not just of devotion but also, it was believed, of healing.

Above: Pilgrims have been coming to Whitchurch Canonicorum for over 1000 years.

St Wite's shrine has been maintained, clandestinely for a period, for 1000 years. How it escaped desecration is a mystery, but somehow it did and when movement in the church wall caused a crack to open in the shrine in 1899, the interior was examined. Inside was a lead reliquary bearing a Latin inscription which translates as 'Here rest the relics of St Wite'. It contained the bones of a small woman who would have been around 40 when she died.

St Thomas More wrote that St Wite's pilgrims brought offerings of cake and cheese to this shrine. If a miracle was performed, the healed person would call 'measure me for St Wite' and a wick the length of the cured part was made into a candle equal to its breadth. If the whole body had been cured, the wick would be woven into a coil or *trindle* before it was coated with wax. A forest of curiously shaped candles grew up around the tomb.

Below: St Wite's shrine, showing the holes where pilgrims seeking a cure placed afflicted limbs.

Lyme Regis – and a secular saint

From Whitchurch to Charmouth the scenery undergoes another radical change. You walk here through lush meadows beside the River Char before a long climb up through Charmouth brings you out above Lyme Regis, and the reward of a grand view of the town laid out beneath you.

Towards the end of the descent you reach St Michael the Archangel church where a local secular saint is remembered: Thomas Coram. Coram was born in Coombe St in 1668, went to sea at 11 and then settled in America. When he returned to England in 1720, he was appalled to see so many abandoned children living on the streets of London. He fought for decades to establish a 'hospital for the maintenance and education of exposed and destitute young children', gained the support of Charles Dickens and William Hogarth, and created the Foundling Hospital at a site in Bloomsbury, London now known as Coram's Fields.

Here in Lyme Regis, the stained-glass Coram Window in the porch of St Michael the Archangel pays tribute to him. The author John Fowles, who lived in Lyme until his death in 2005, wrote of him: 'Dear old Coram died in 1751, a complete pauper. Every penny of his fortune had been 'lost' in the hospital. Lyme has more famous names attached to it, but none of kinder memory.'

My journey complete, I lounge on The Cobb, the harbour wall on which Fowles's *French Lieutenant's Woman* risks a watery fate in the book and film, and reflect on an extraordinary journey that has taken me from the (literal) heights of St Catherine's Chapel via the bloody lows of Chideock's Martyr's Church, and the extraordinary shrine to St Wite at Whitchurch Canonicorum, to this pleasant spot. For me, this has been one of the finest pilgrimages.

Above: The Coram Window, St Michael's Church, Lyme Regis

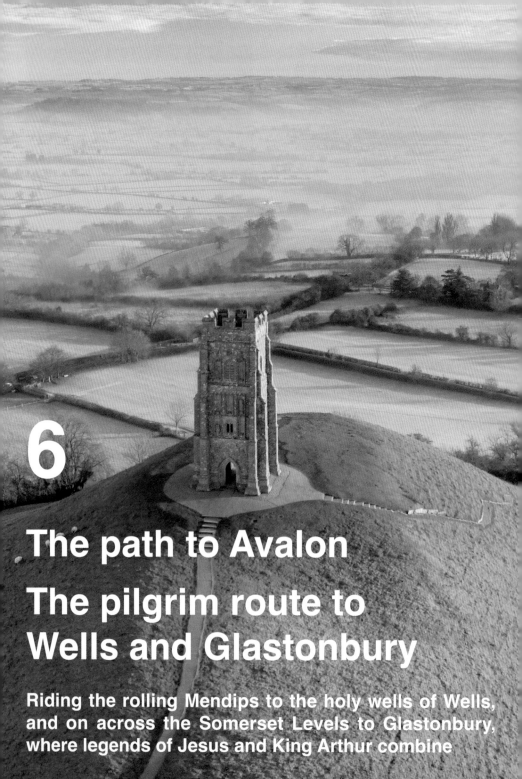

6

The path to Avalon

The pilgrim route to Wells and Glastonbury

Riding the rolling Mendips to the holy wells of Wells, and on across the Somerset Levels to Glastonbury, where legends of Jesus and King Arthur combine

All day long the sky has been hanging low and heavy like a saturated, ominously bulging ceiling about to burst. Now, as I catch my first distant glimpse of Glastonbury Tor, pointing its pin-prick tower at the sky, I wonder if it is about to pop heaven's balloon.

I am still some way from Wells, the half-way point of this pilgrimage, yet my final destination is already hovering on the horizon. Is it taunting me with how many miles I still have to travel? Or acting as a beacon, guiding me forward? That, I am snowflake enough to admit, all depends on what the weather has in store.

Glastonbury Tor

PRACTICAL INFORMATION

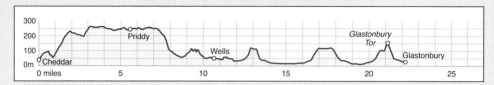

- **Terrain** A mix of grassy paths, woodland tracks and quiet lanes
- **Difficulty** Generally moderate with challenging stretches
- **Directions & GPS*** 006.pdf, 006.gpx, 006.kml at 🖥 https://trailblazer-guides.com/press

* See p10-11 for more information on downloads

ROUTE OVERVIEW   22 miles (35.5km)

Although this is a challenging landscape at times, the rewards are ample for both pilgrims and nature lovers. Make sure you have plenty of food and water with you for the Wells to Glastonbury stretch.

Cheddar to Wells   10.6 miles (17km)

- **Time** 4hrs 45mins actual walking time
- **Total ascent** 751m/2464ft
- **Map** OS Explorer *141 Cheddar Gorge & Mendip Hills West*

The route climbs out of Cheddar and soon joins the West Mendip Way, reasonably well signposted with its white-arrow-on-blue roundels, which it follows to Wells, with a couple of short diversions. The path descends to Bradley Cross **(0.9 miles)** before climbing again to pass through Draycott Sleights Nature Reserve **(1.2 miles)** then runs along the top of the Mendip Hills to Priddy **(3.3 miles)**, before descending to Wookey Hole **(3.2 miles)** and reaching Wells in **2 miles**.

Wells to Glastonbury   11.4 miles (18.5km)

- **Time** 4hrs 30mins actual walking time
- **Total ascent** 459m/1506ft
- **Map** OS Explorer *141 Cheddar Gorge & Mendip Hills West*

Today's walk follows The Monarch's Way, reasonably well signposted with roundels depicting a sailing ship and an oak tree, from Wells over rolling hills via North Wootton **(3.6 miles)** to shortly before West Pennard, reached in **4.2 miles**. From here the going is very flat, on footpaths over meadows, until the steep ascent to Glastonbury Tor **(2.6 miles)** and final descent to Glastonbury Abbey, reached in **1 mile**.

Day walk options

Start at Wells, reaching Glastonbury in a day.

- **By public transport** The nearest railway station to Wells and Glastonbury is Castle Cary, from where you can take a taxi, or take the train to Bristol and a bus from there.

● **Taxi option** Craigs Taxi Service (☎ 07563-612473, 💻 taxisincastle cary.co.uk)

Where to eat or stay
● **Cheddar** Stay at Gordons Hotel (☎ 01934-742497, 💻 gor donshotel.co.uk, Cliff St), a friendly, family-run hotel in the centre of town.
● **Priddy Eat** lunch at the *Queen Victoria* (☎ 01749-676385, 💻 the queenvicpriddy.co.uk, Pelting Drove; Mon-Fri noon-3pm & 5-9pm, Sat noon-9pm, Sun noon-8pm) a lovely village pub on the summit of the Mendips.
● **Wells Stay** at the *Ancient Gatehouse Hotel* (☎ 01749-672 029, 💻 ancientgatehouse.com, 20 Sadler St) which backs on to Cathedral Green, and **eat** in their

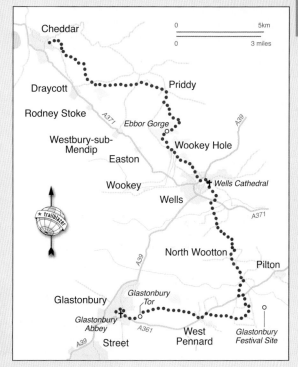

Rugantino's restaurant (food: Sun, Mon & Thur noon-2.30pm & 6.30-8.30pm, Fri & Sat noon-2.30pm & 5.30-8pm, Tue & Wed closed).
● **Glastonbury Eat** at the *George and Pilgrim's Hotel* (☎ 01458-831146, 💻 historicinnz .co.uk/glastonbury, 1 High St; food served daily from 5pm).

PILGRIMAGE HIGHLIGHTS

● Climb the **Mendip Hills** for a high-wire walk through an ancient landscape.
● Explore **Wells Cathedral** (💻 wellscathedral.org.uk; 10am-4pm) and **Bishop's Palace** (💻 bishopspalace.org.uk; Apr-Oct 10am-6pm, Nov-Mar 10am-4pm.)
● Scale the heights of **Glastonbury Tor** then drink the holy waters at the **Chalice Well** (☎ 01458-831154, 💻 chalicewell.org.uk, 85-89 Chilkwell St; Apr-Oct 10am-6pm, Nov-Mar 10am-4.30pm).
● Explore the legends at **Glastonbury Abbey** (💻 glastonburyabbey.com, Magda-lene St; 9am-5pm.)

Glastonbury pilgrimages
Anglican celebrations on a Saturday in the second half of June,
Catholic on a Sunday in early July (💻 glastonburyabbey.com)

Above: Looking back towards Cheddar.

Cheddar to Priddy

The threat of rain has been with me right from the initial climb from Cheddar via Bradley Cross to the old pilgrim route along the broad back of the Mendip Hills. But that threat has been tempered with hints of a more clement outcome. Once I am high enough to see across to the distant coast at Weston-super-Mare, a few isolated patches of far-away sun offer me encouragement.

The Mendips are a stark and primal landscape: all skin and bone. The limestone has broken through the green skin of grass, pimpled with brown molehills, at Draycott Sleights Nature Reserve. Yet, depending on the time you visit, the grasslands will be sparkling with cowslips, wild marjoram, wild thyme or bee orchids. Ground nesting meadow pipits and skylarks might flit from beneath your feet.

Up here, there are tumuli, earthworks and barrows all around. Even the stiles in the drystone walls – great tablets of stone laid on edge – feel like ancient burial slabs. But, with the rain holding off, there is nothing gloomy about the landscape as I stride along the top of the world, on a die-straight route to the village of Priddy, and lunch.

Priddy really is ancient. There is a stone circle near here which, at around 4000 years old, is a contemporary of Stonehenge. The Romans mined lead, leaving mounds known locally as 'gruffy ground', and there has been a sheep fair on Priddy village green since 1348.

There is also a remarkable legend, which asserts that the young Jesus came here with his tin-dealer uncle, Joseph of Arimathea, coming because Priddy was at the centre of a copper (used with tin in the manufacture of bronze) and lead-mining area. An age-old local proverb runs: 'As sure as our Lord was at Priddy', and a folk song includes the lines:

'O Joseph came a-sailing over the sea,

A-trading of metal, a-trading came he

And he made his way to Priddy

With our dear Lord.'

Ebbor Gorge and Wookey Hole

Winding down the southern scarp of the Mendips to the Ebbor Gorge National Nature Reserve, the day darkens again, but the white stars of wood anemones are like cats' eyes, leading me through the ash and oak to the edge of the limestone cliffs, where there is another panoramic view.

As the path descends to Hope Wood Valley, and runs

alongside a stream, things get decidedly steamy. This area is renowned for its humidity, in which ferns and fungi thrive. Around 250 species of moss, liverwort and lichen, many rare, have been recorded here.

Then comes the descent to Wookey Hole, a jarringly touristy hotspot after my walk through wild nature. The village's remarkable sequence of limestone show caves have been augmented with all the trappings of a family resort. The car parks are packed and the queue for ice creams

daunting. On the far side of the village, at Lime Kiln Lane, I get that first inspiring view of Glastonbury Tor on the horizon and, below me, the city of Wells.

Wells Cathedral and Bishop's Palace

St Andrew's is a remarkable building, even by the high standards of English cathedrals. You approach via the west front and are faced with rank upon rank of medieval stone figures. These – 300 of the original 400 have survived – are a sort of Who's

Below: The magnificent West Front of Wells Cathedral, constructed between 1175 and 1255.

Who of the Christian faith or, as one 19th century archaeologist put it, 'a calendar for unlearned men'.

The doctrines and history of Christianity are illustrated here, in a roll call of prophets, saints, princes, bishops, and the missionaries who brought the faith to these islands. Christ himself stands up on the gable. Imagine this as it once was, the figures brightly painted. Suddenly coming upon it as you walked through the narrow archway into the cathedral precincts would be akin to experiencing a vision.

Go inside and they have a suggestion: 'Be a pilgrim – for just 10 minutes.' A leaflet guides you round the Stations of the Cross, 14 panels depicting the key stages on Jesus's final journey to his crucifixion. The Stations aren't common in Anglican churches, but feature in every Catholic one. To walk and pray them is a mini pilgrimage in itself.

Next door, behind its walls and moat, is the 13th century Bishop's Palace, where 14 acres of immaculately kept gardens are alive with the sound of water, running in rivulets and torrents, and bubbling up from the wells that give the city its name. This is a perfect place for further reflection.

Wells is also the ideal place for an overnight stay, with a cluster of venerable old hotels around the cathedral. Despite its diminutive size, honeyed-stone Wells has been a city since medieval times, thanks to that remarkable cathedral. It's a pleasant place to wander around, with good cafés around the Market Place and a wonderful foodie market every Saturday and Wednesday. I pick up the ingredients for a picnic lunch for tomorrow.

Above: Vicars' Close, said to be the oldest continually-occupied medieval street in Europe.
Top: The scissor arches in Wells Cathedral were built in 1383-48 to support the tower.

THE WELLS OF WELLS

The clue is in the name: there would be no Wells without the wells. The waters that surge to the surface here are the reason the city exists. They rise from an underground river which originates on the Mendip Hills, a point proven in 1930 when a geologist put dye in potholes on the tops and, a few days later, the wells turned green.

Above: St Andrew's Well in the gardens of the Bishop's Palace.

The ceaselessly flowing waters from these wells might be seen as reflecting the perfect City of God in the Book of Revelation: 'Then the angel showed me the river of life, rising from the throne of God and flowing crystal clear. Down the middle of the city street, on either side of the river, were the trees of life, the leaves of which are for the healing of the nations.'

In 1451 Bishop Beckynton set up a well house to pump water to the market square, just outside the palace gates, for the use of townsfolk. The surplus was channelled through gullies and was used to wash away blood and offal from the butchers' stalls. The gullies are still there, though the offal is not. The market has a decidedly more crafty feel these days.

The Somerset Levels

From Wells I cross the flats, emerging from Park Wood to see Glastonbury Tor again. It proves to be a marker that will guide me today, periodically popping up through the clouds as I cross the Somerset Levels. Yet it is a curiously inconsistent beacon. Seen again at the village of North Wootton it seems smaller than before, at other times it swells, harvest-moon like.

Climbing Pennard Hill, an island in the levels, I pass an ancient apple orchard where the trees are hung with great orbs of mistletoe and, walking to the east of the village of Pilton, reach Worthy Lane, on the edge of the Glastonbury Festival site at Worthy Farm. I picnic on the heights before making the descent to the village of West Pennard, after which I am on the home straight, making good time over lush water meadows.

Right: Glastonbury Tor

The final approach to Glastonbury from Norwood Park Farm takes me up a back lane, to reach the Tor on the opposite side from the crocodile of visitors tramping up from Glastonbury town.

Glastonbury

The Tor has been a place of pilgrimage since prehistoric times. It may be the summit of the Isle of Avalon of Arthurian legend and placing a Christian church here was a very powerful visual statement of

appropriation, visible for many miles around. St Michael's Tower is all that remains of a church which fell into ruin when Glastonbury Abbey was pillaged at the Reformation.

The Tor is also a site of martyrdom: Glastonbury's abbot, Richard Whyting, was dragged here by horses after he refused to surrender the abbey, and was hanged, drawn and quartered.

I take a moment to sweep the panoramic view, yet find achieving the summit strangely anticlimactic. Along the way, the views of the Tor have been so powerful that this one, which inevitably excludes it, is of a lesser landscape.

At the foot of the Tor I take in the Chalice Well, where the waters rise to the well head with a rumble like a cistern filling. The way these iron-rich waters stain the

Above: The Chalice Well

cascade, rill and healing pool through which they tumble led to this once being known as the Blood Spring.

There is a legend of the Holy Grail here, which holds that these waters represent the blood of Christ, and that they spring miraculously from the ground where Joseph of Arimathea buried or washed the cup – the chalice from which the well takes its name – used at the Last Supper.

I fill a bottle at the lion's head drinking fountain while a group of women discard their wellies and dip their feet in the pool. We are doing what pilgrims have done here for many centuries.

Then it's on into town, past – or possibly into – the George and Pilgrim's Hotel, and round the corner to Glastonbury Abbey. Just inside the entrance is an unassuming-looking tree with a powerful

KING ARTHUR, JOSEPH OF ARIMATHEA AND JESUS

There are two great legends associated with Glastonbury. The first is that the abbey was founded by St Joseph of Arimathea in the 1st century, and that he visited the site with the young Jesus, his nephew, making this the cradle of English Christianity. In the 12th century, a second legend brought another towering figure into the story: King Arthur.

Arthur, according to myth, was a 5th and early 6th century British king who defended the land against Saxon invaders. His connection with Glastonbury originates, by one account, from a tale told by a Welsh bard to Henry II. The bard said Arthur and his queen, Guinevere, were buried here. Excavations in the abbey graveyard uncovered a great oak coffin buried 16ft (5m) down. It lay beneath a lead cross bearing an inscription which read, in Latin: 'Here lies the famous King Arthur on the Isle of Avalon'. It contained two skeletons.

The remains were reburied beneath the high altar in the abbey church, making veneration of Arthur indistinguishable from Christian observance.

name: the Holy Thorn. It is another part of the legend of Joseph of Arimathea's visit with Jesus. It flowers – unusually – twice a year, once in winter on new wood, once in spring on old, and is said to be the latest in a long line of cuttings, the first taken from a staff that Joseph staked into the ground here, and which grew.

The ruins are a mere shadow of what, in the 14th century, was a Christian site surpassed only by Westminster Abbey, but you can still piece together its story. There is the chapel dedicated to St Joseph, the biblical donor of Christ's tomb, where sick pilgrims came in hope of a cure; the site of King Arthur's tomb, standing between the two pillars that once supported a great Gothic arch; and, more prosaically, the Abbot's Kitchen, which has survived intact as a very rare example of a medieval kitchen.

I take a perch beside the Holy Thorn and reflect on this pilgrimage. Glastonbury Tor has to be one of the most instantly recognisable sites in the world. So much so that, when the government ran post-Covid TV ads to try to winkle us out of lockdown, an aerial shot of it was one of the kaleidoscope of attractions they sought to tempt us with. It is the logical highlight of this walk, but I also treasure the less showy delights – such as Priddy, the Chalice Well and, as I discover when I pop in later, the George and Pilgrim's Hotel. As its name would suggest, it offers the perfect restoratives for the weary pilgrim.

Below: The ruins of Glastonbury Abbey

SITE OF KING ARTHUR'S TOMB. IN THE YEAR 1191 THE BODIES OF KING ARTHUR AND HIS QUEEN WERE SAID TO HAVE BEEN FOUND ON THE SOUTH SIDE OF THE LADY CHAPEL. ON 19TH APRIL 1278 THEIR REMAINS WERE REMOVED IN THE PRESENCE OF KING EDWARD I AND QUEEN ELEANOR TO A BLACK MARBLE TOMB ON THIS SITE. THIS TOMB SURVIVED UNTIL THE DISSOLUTION OF THE ABBEY IN 1539

SITE OF THE ANCIENT GRAVEYARD WHERE IN 1191 THE MONKS DUG TO FIND THE TOMBS OF ARTHUR AND GUINEVERE

7

The Cornish Saints' Way
Padstow to Fowey

A trail from sea to shining sea on the ancient pilgrim route that spans Cornwall

There's something special about travelling coast to coast. Walking across Cornwall from sea to shining sea may not have the same sense of heroic adventure as, say, crossing America, but it is still a stirring experience. To leave the Camel Estuary behind you one fine morning and find the waters of the River Fowey welcoming you two afternoons later is the perfect beginning and end to your journey. But what of the middle?

The middle is the Saints' Way. Long before it became the route for monks from Wales and Ireland to spread the Christian message throughout Cornwall, and for pilgrims bound for Compostela, Rome or Jerusalem, it was known as the Drovers' Way. For millennia, herdsmen and traders from Wales and Ireland walked it, as keen as pilgrims to avoid the perilous sea journey around Land's End.

The Saints' Way serves up the moors of St Breock Downs and rocky heights of Helman Tor, a string of lovely villages, holy wells, standing stones and wayside Celtic crosses.

Lane after St Breoch

PRACTICAL INFORMATION

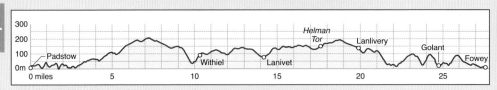

- **Terrain** Footpaths, farm tracks and quiet lanes with sustained uphill sections. Short sections on A and B roads.
- **Difficulty** Challenging
- **Directions & GPS*** 007.pdf, 007.gpx, 007.kml at 🖥 https://trailblazer-guides.com/press

  * See p10-11 for more information on downloads

ROUTE OVERVIEW   27.6 miles (44.4km)

Be prepared for plenty of climbing and descending. The highest parts of the walk are exposed and often windy so check the weather forecast and ensure you are properly equipped with the appropriate clothing. Take a packed lunch for the Padstow to Lanivet section.

Padstow to Lanivet   14.3 miles (23km)

- **Time** 5hrs 45mins actual walking time ● **Total ascent** 625m/2050ft
- **Map** OS Explorer *106 Newquay & Padstow; 107 St Austell & Liskeard*

The route picks up the Saints' Way at St Petroc, Padstow and climbs alongside the River Camel to reach Little Petherick **(2.5 miles)**. You follow the Saints' Way, extremely well marked with black Celtic Crosses, all the way to Fowey. There is a steady but fairly gentle climb to St Breock Downs **(5.1 miles)** followed by a slow descent via Tregustick **(2 miles)** and Withiel **(0.8 mile)** to Lanivet, reached in a further **3.9 miles**.

Lanivet to Fowey   13.3 miles (21.4km)

- **Time** 5hrs 15mins actual walking time ● **Total ascent** 704m/2309ft
- **Map** OS Explorer *107 St Austell & Liskeard*

The second part of the walk begins with a steady, occasionally strenuous climb to Helman Tor **(3.5 miles)** followed by a long slow descent via Lanlivery **(1.9 miles)** to Milltown **(2.5 miles)**. Then comes a further climb and descent to Golant, reached in **2.2 miles**, before the final stretch high above the River Fowey to Fowey itself **(3.2 miles)**.

Day walk options

- **By public transport** For the Padstow to Lanivet section, take a train to Bodmin Parkway station, then a taxi to Padstow. From Lanivet take a taxi back to Bodmin Parkway station. For Lanivet to Fowey, from Bodmin Parkway station take a taxi to Lanivet. From the end point at Fowey, take a bus or taxi to Par station for a train home.
- **Taxi option** Carbis Cabs (☎ 07944-034547, 🖥 bodmin-parkway-taxis.co.uk).

Where to eat or stay along the way

● **Padstow Stay** overnight in Padstow at the *Old Custom House* (☎ 01841-532359, 🖥️ oldcustomhousepadstow.co.uk, S. Quay) right on the harbour.

● **Lanivet Stay** at *St Benet's Abbey* (☎ 01208-831352, 🖥️ stbenetsabbey.co.uk, Truro Rd), a 15th century former pilgrim hostelry turned B&B. **Eat** at the *Lanivet Inn* (☎ 01208-831212, 🖥️ lanivetinn.co.uk; food Mon-Sat noon-2.30pm & 5-9pm, Sun noon-9pm) for superior, locally sourced and seasonal pub grub.

● **Lanlivery Eat lunch** at the *Crown Inn* (☎ 01208-872707, 🖥️ thecrowninncornwall .co.uk), a pilgrim hostelry dating from 1130. Food daily noon-2.30pm & 6-8.30pm.

● **Fowey Eat** at *The Old Quay House* (☎ 01726-833302, 🖥️ theoldquayhouse.com, 28 Fore St), where you can sample their Fowey River oysters, local scallops, or fabulous fish and chips. Food daily noon-2.30pm & 6-9pm.

PILGRIMAGE HIGHLIGHTS

● Visit St Petroc's churches in **Padstow** (🖥 padstowparishchurch.org.uk), site of his 6th century abbey, and **Little Petherick** (🖥 padstowparishchurch.org.uk) where he retreated into nature.

● Enjoy spectacular views from high above the **Camel Estuary**, at **St Breock Downs** and **Helman Tor**.

● Seek out the peace of **St Clement's, Withiel** and **St Nivet's, Lanivet** (🖥 achurchnearyou.com/church/2487/) with its towering Celtic crosses.

● Explore **St Sampson's** church near **Golant** (🖥 achurchnearyou.com/church/2475) with its holy well, and **St Fimbarrus** in **Fowey** (🖥 foweyparishchurch.org, 5 Church Ave)

Saint's feast days: St Petroc 4 June; St Finnbar 25 September.

Padstow

This is going to be a perfect day. It just doesn't know it yet. The sea mist hasn't decided whether to burn off now or block out the sun for another hour or two, but I know all will come good. In Padstow harbour, there is not a ripple on the water, not a trace of a breeze.

From all the places around town that bear his name, you might think Padstow's patron was St Stein but, while Rick and his many food businesses are ubiquitous today, it was St Petroc who put the town on the pilgrim map. The Saints' Way begins at the lych gate of Padstow's parish church, which is dedicated to the saint.

Petroc built his monastery here, in an area defined by the present churchyard, though the only reminders of it are a Celtic cross beside the doorway, and the stump of another by the lower gate. There is a further reminder of medieval pilgrimage in Abbey House, which stands beside Padstow's harbour on North Quay. In the 15th century, this was a pilgrim hostelry.

As I climb out of town, the Camel Estuary shimmers, its waters eggshell blue, the sand dunes across the river a pastel sketch of perfection. The way narrows: the road becomes a lane, then track, finally a footpath, drawing me ever deeper into the peace of the countryside. You get a different perspective on things in Cornwall. Here, the stones in the dry-stone walls are stacked vertically, rather than horizontally, sometimes in a jaunty herringbone pattern. At the top of Dennis Hill, one of these sideways walls is supplemented by a sideways fence, the posts sticking out horizontally.

Above: The Saints' Way begins at St Petroc's church in Padstow.
Below: Padstow harbour.

ST PETROC

St Petroc was a Welsh nobleman who joined an Irish monastery. In 518 he landed as a missionary to the Cornish at Trebetherick, on the eastern shore of the Camel Estuary, with a small group of followers.

He is often portrayed with a stag, a reference to the legend that by protecting a deer being hunted by Constantine of Dumnonia, whose kingdom covered modern Cornwall and Devon, he converted the king to Christianity.

The name Padstow comes from St Petroc's town. He stayed here for 30 years, but went on pilgrimages to Rome and Jerusalem, probably following the Saints'

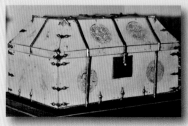

Way. He died in 564 and was buried at Padstow. His monastery was destroyed by Viking raiders in 981 and his remains taken by the fleeing monks to Bodmin, where Petroc had also established a monastery. The decorated ivory *reliquary* (casket, **photo left**) that contained his remains is in St Petroc's church in Padstow.

Little Petherick

The mudflats are gleaming like melted chocolate as I begin my descent to the village of Little Petherick. Down at ground level, opposite Creekside Holiday Cottages, a stream tumbles into what was St Petroc's Well. Petroc is said to have moved here from Padstow, and lived an austere life surviving on bread and water, with porridge on Sundays, and immersing himself up to the neck in Little Petherick Creek while chanting psalms.

Petroc came here with 12 companions, to live in what was then named Nansfonteyn, or 'valley with a spring'. Petroc built a chapel, on the site of the present 14th century parish church, which stands alongside the path.

I push open the churchyard gate to find a great, coffin-shaped stone wedged between the gate and the steps up to the church, as if some long-gone pall bearers found they could heave it no further. Looking up to the tower I see crows nests in the

Below: Little Petherick Creek at low tide.

Above: Little Petherick church.

Above: St Breock Longstone.

slatted openings, above an angel carved in stone. Inside, this sombre church is a surprise: it is as brightly painted as a Victorian merry-go-round.

Then comes a brief encounter with the A389 before I peel off onto a stream-side path to Mellingey, a quiet lane to Trenance, and on to the ancient settlement at Blable House, once a perilous place for pilgrims. The name comes from Blyth-Poll, meaning wolf pit.

St Breock Downs

The climb to St Breock Downs is rewarded with spectacular views right back to the Camel Estuary. Up here, the wind thrums the telephone wires and great giant wind turbines turn with a fwump, fwump. If the

exertion of the morning's climb has dampened your shirt, the breeze here will dry it – fast.

At the summit is St Breock Longstone, the largest and heaviest prehistoric standing stone in Cornwall, 3m/12ft tall and weighing 16.5 tonnes. This was once a significant meeting place, and its Cornish name is Men Gurta – stone of waiting. From here I exchange the view back for the view ahead, and dip down, off the grassy tops, through the hamlet of Tregustick to the bottom of the valley, where I find the first stream I have seen since Little Petherick. This is the Ruthern River, once stained red by the tin mining that took place upstream. There is a footbridge alongside the

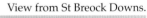

View from St Breock Downs.

7

Above: The lichen-covered church at Withiel.

Above: The former St Benet's Abbey, Lanivet.

ford, but I choose to wade across. It's only a couple of inches on the ridge of smaller stones that forms an arc across, and cooling and soothing on the feet.

Withiel to Lanivet

There are two lovely churches on this last leg of the first day's walk. First comes 13th century St Clement's at Withiel, with its belt of ancient yews along the churchyard boundary.

The stone is covered with white and sage-green lichen, which gives the church a furry appearance, as if nature is slowly dissolving it. Above the porch door is an ancient sundial, and I check the time it points to against my watch. Add an hour for summer time and it's right: 12.30.

At Teremorebridge, a spring feeds a well by the road. It has no saint attached, and the water looks a little murky as it tumbles into its round trough. I dip my fingers in nevertheless, before tackling the final approach to Lanivet, and the second of those wonderful churches.

Above: Lanivet Celtic cross

Lanivet

The name Lanivet reveals both the Christian and the pagan heritage in this village. It comes from 'Lann', meaning 'church site' in Cornish, and 'neved' meaning 'a pagan sacred place'.

Christianity arrived in the 5th century, when St Nivet, daughter of the Welsh king, Brychan, settled here, and the village church is dedicated to her.

In the churchyard are two towering Celtic crosses: one from the 13th century by a yew to the left of the church porch; the other from the 10th century in the graveyard behind the church, with a chunk taken out of its head. This is said to be the most elaborately carved in Cornwall, and to show a man with a tail or, possibly, an unidentified saint with a key on a chain. Now, I like to try to use my imagination, but no amount of peering at this cross revealed either man, tail, saint or key. Just a very time-worn abstract pattern.

The other significant pilgrim place in Lanivet is on the

edge of the village. St Benet's Abbey, now a B&B, was built as a Benedictine monastery in 1411. The emblem of St John of Jerusalem on the end wall reveals it was administered by the Knights Hospitallers, founded in 1144 to care for pilgrims, and is evidence that it also gave shelter to those following the Saints' Way, as it does again today.

Lanivet to Helman Tor

The next day begins with a climb out of the village, under the A30 and past the wayside crosses at Reperry Cross and St Ingunger, where once there was a chapel and holy well.

My next landmark, Helman Tor, pops up on the horizon, and as I get closer I make out the great boulders that balance precariously at several points on the

Above: Wall Pennywort thrives in Cornwall.

210m/680ft rocky summit. Scramble up and you will find remnants of a prehistoric hill fort and settlement dating back 6000 years, and views – on a clear day – back to the Atlantic coast to the north and on to the Channel to the south.

The Saints' Way divides just before Helman Tor, and I have chosen to take the eastern option, because I want to come into Fowey along the river. The other option runs via the villages of Luxulyan and St Blazey to Fowey, missing out the stretch along the Fowey estuary, which I consider one of the highlights of the walk. My route follows a granite-lined ridgeway running to Lanlivery under spreading oaks, the verges verdant with a fine display of purple foxgloves, red campion and ferns.

THE AGE OF THE SAINTS

Cornwall probably has more saints than any other county. Many are very local, and devotion to them survived the Reformation to thrive today. They have their roots in the period of turmoil following the end of Roman occupation of Britain, a time known as the Age of the Saints.

From 450 to 600 – a period of war, threat and uncertainty – the Celts of Cornwall were receptive to the Christian message. While many religious figures were pilgrims passing through, some became missionaries, roaming Cornwall and evangelising. Many Cornish saints were

St Petroc

Welsh, reputed to be the descendants of King Brychan of Brecon, others from Ireland.

Cornwall has three patron saints: St Petroc, St Piran and St Michael. St Piran is the patron saint of tin miners and his flag, a white cross on a black background, is also the county emblem. St Michael, patron saint of fishermen, is associated with St Michael's Mount, on the southern coast of the county.

Above: Standing stone and view to St Brevita's.

Lanlivery

In the distance I see my next landmark: St Brevita's church in Lanlivery, its tower topped with four spikes rather like minarets. Here in the Cornish countryside, church towers still dominate as they once did in every town and city across the land.

John Betjeman called St Brevita's 'one of the great churches of Cornwall', and I'd like to add an honourable mention for the equally pleasing pub across the lane: The Crown Inn, a medieval long house dating from 1130. This was once the final overnight stop for drovers taking their animals to Fowey, where they would be shipped onward, and no doubt also for pilgrims.

Rested and revived, I press on, passing a standing stone in a meadow just beyond Pelyn Tor Cottage. When I look back to St Brevita's, I see the church and the standing stone have been designed to do exactly the same: they point to heaven.

Milltown to Golant

A short stretch on the verge of the A390 brings the wider world intruding for a few minutes before the Saints' Way plunges back into the countryside, passing through the village of Milltown and then running parallel with the River Fowey, and offering glimpses of its cool waters through the woods that fringe it.

Just before the village of Golant, beside Penquite farm, comes St Sampson's church and Holy Well. St Sampson was archbishop of Dol in Brittany in the 6th century. It is said he stayed in or near Golant when travelling from Ireland to France, as did many other Cornish saints.

To the left of the porch is St Sampson's Holy Well, looking like a little stone dog kennel. I am disappointed to find that the well is dry, and suddenly feel very thirsty. I notice a tap on the wall nearby. Perfect. It turns, but no water comes. St Sampson's tap, like his well, is dry.

Next comes a dip down into Golant, a little fishing place on the riverbank. The village, like the cat lazing on a windowsill, is asleep in the sun, the boats on the river just turning with the tide. From here it is a short walk through the woods, and a punishing climb, before the final coast down into Fowey.

Above: St Sampson's Holy Well, near Golant.

Fowey

Fowey: rhymes with joy. Say it like that and you'll pass for a local. The route passes the little ferry that takes cars and passengers across to Bodinnick, on along the narrow, winding main street where a fast approaching van has me leaping into a doorway.

There is an echo of pilgrimage here, in the 18th century Scallop Shell House on Custom House Hill, built on the spot where once pilgrims rested before boarding a ship for Santiago, Rome, or Jerusalem. A large scallop shell decorates the canopy above the front door.

More winding through town brings me to 15th century St Fimbarrus church. Like you, St Finbarr arrived in Fowey along the Saints' Way. A 7th century bishop of Cork, he had intended a pilgrimage to Rome but stayed and founded a Christian community. The original Saxon church is long gone, and several rebuilds – the last in the 19th century – have bequeathed Fowey a

Fowey – Above: Scallop Shell House. Below: St Fimbarrus and the River Fowey.

very grand church. It still has its Norman font though, a 500-year-old waggon/barrel vaulted roof and a pulpit made 400 years ago with timbers from a Spanish galleon.

I end my journey sitting on the riverside, looking out over Fowey's harbour. OK, so I haven't crossed a continent, but I have gone from coast to coast, and that adds a sense of achievement out of proportion to the effort involved, but entirely in keeping with the spirit of pilgrimage.

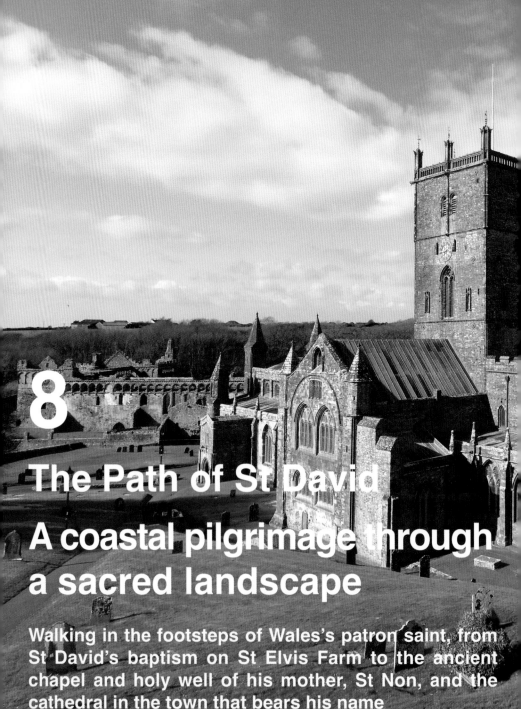

8

The Path of St David

A coastal pilgrimage through a sacred landscape

Walking in the footsteps of Wales's patron saint, from St David's baptism on St Elvis Farm to the ancient chapel and holy well of his mother, St Non, and the cathedral in the town that bears his name

It is hard to believe that St Elvis Farm was once a significant place of pilgrimage. More than that: it's hard to believe that there really was a St Elvis. Yet there was and, even more remarkably, he is said to have baptised the far-better known St David, patron saint of Wales, right here, in the waters of the holy well that bubbles up near the white-washed farmhouse.

In the muddy farmyard is a distinctive barn which was built, in the 20th century, from dressed stone taken from a demolished church dedicated to St Elvis. Today, St David's shrine in the cathedral city that bears his name is once again a place of pilgrimage, yet the well and former church at St Elvis Farm, and their history as a place of veneration, are almost completely forgotten.

St David's Cathedral

PRACTICAL INFORMATION

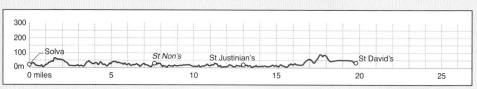

- **Terrain** Mainly coastal paths, occasionally rocky and uneven, with steep ascents and descents. Short stretch on quiet lanes.
- **Difficulty** Challenging
- **Directions & GPS*** 008.pdf, 008.gpx, 008.kml at
  🖥 https://trailblazer-guides.com/press
  * See p10-11 for more information on downloads

ROUTE OVERVIEW   19.8 miles (31.8km)

You could easily base yourself in the tiny city of St Davids for both legs of this coastal walk and divide it up at other locations if you wish, as it loops round the headland. You might want to take your binoculars as there are fabulous bird-spotting opportunities.

Solva to St Non's via St Elvis Farm   7.7 miles (12.4km)

- **Time** 3 hours actual walking time
- **Total ascent** 705m / 2312ft
- **Map** OS Explorer *OL35 North Pembrokeshire*

The first part of the route is a circuit from Solva, initially following the generally well-signposted Pembrokeshire Coast Path, to St Elvis Farm, reached in **1.7 miles,** returning to Solva in a further **1.2 miles.**

From Solva you follow the coast path again, alternating between long cliff top sections interspersed with short, sharp descents to cross narrow inlets and corresponding climbs, to reach St Non's in **4.8 miles.**

St Non's to St David's Cathedral   12.1 miles (19.4km)

- **Time** 5hrs 15mins actual walking time
- **Total ascent** 352m / 1154ft
- **Map** OS Explorer *OL35 North Pembrokeshire*

From St Non's the route follows the Pembrokeshire Coast Path, again mainly along clifftops, with periodic descents and ascents to cross inlets, via the narrow harbour at Porthclais **(1.2 miles)** to St Justinian's, with its lifeboat stations **(4.4 miles).** From here, the path descends gently to cross behind the sandy beach at Whitesands Bay **(2.2 miles)** and then climb steadily to the rocky landscape at St David's Head **(1.1 miles).**

From St David's Head you leave the coastal path to swing inland, descending gently to cross farmland on the approach to St Davids, reached in **3.2 miles.**

Day walk options

To complete this walk in a day, start at St Non's. If you're in a car, park in St Davids and walk from there directly to St Non's (about 0.8miles) to begin the walk.

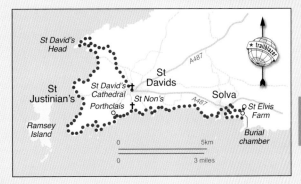

● **By public transport** Take a train to Haverfordwest, then a bus to St Davids or taxi directly to St Non's to start the walk. At the end of the day, take a bus or taxi from St Davids back to Haverfordwest.

● **Taxi option** Clarks Taxis (☎ 01437 710077, ⌨ clarkstaxis.co.uk)

Where to eat or stay along the way

● **Solva Stay** at the *Ship Inn* (☎ 01437-721528, ⌨ theshipinnsolva.co.uk, 15 Main St), a walker-friendly village pub. Pick up the ingredients for a **picnic lunch** from *Bayview Stores* (☎ 01437-729554, ⌨ bayviewstores.co.uk, 19 Maes Ewan; 7am-7pm) to enjoy on your cliff-top walk, perhaps sampling their local crab and lobster.

● **Whitesands Bay** Have a picnic **lunch** on the beach, or in the *Whitesands Bay Café* (☎ 01437-720068; SA62 6PS; Summer: Mon-Sat 10.30am-5.30pm, Sun 11am-4pm; Winter weekends only) which is renowned for its fish & chips and toasted sandwiches.

● **St Davids Stay** 0.7miles from St Non's with *St Davids Kitchen* (☎ 01437-720404, ⌨ stdavidskitchen.co.uk, 16 Nun St), ideally in a room with a view of the cathedral, and **eat** in their restaurant, which specialises in local seasonal produce.

PILGRIMAGE HIGHLIGHTS

● Discover the holy well, former chapel and ancient burial chamber at **St Elvis Farm**, where St David was baptised, and explore his birthplace at **St Non's,** where a chapel and holy well are named after the saint's mother.

● Enjoy views of the bird reserve **Ramsey Island** and take a boat trip to or around it if you have time, booking well ahead with **Thousand Islands Expeditions** (⌨ thousandislands.co.uk, Cross Square, St Davids; 1 Apr-31 Oct)

● Visit **St David's shrine** and end your pilgrimage with Evensong at **St David's Cathedral** (⌨ stdavidscathedral.org.uk; 10am-4pm; Choral Evensong Sun 6pm)

St David's feast day: 1 March

Solva and St Elvis

It is with a sense of embarking on a voyage of discovery that I take the Pembrokeshire Coast Path out of Solva, scrambling up to ride the high ridge that flanks the little harbour, on my way to St Elvis. Looping east like this, before coming round to tack west for the other pilgrim points on the Path of St David, gives a wonderful introduction to a coastal landscape that was sacred to pilgrims.

At the seaward end of the ridge I drop down to cross Gwadyn, a cloistered little beach tiled in large flat pebbles, and cross a stream into which the waters from St Elvis's holy well flow.

Sadly, the footpath that Ordnance Survey maps show crossing St Elvis Farm's yard does not exist on the ground, though you can get very close to this holy site. Still easily

accessible is a 5000-year-old burial chamber, or cromlech, which is another key element in the veneration of St Elvis.

The sick would be bathed in the waters of the holy well, then laid upon the chamber's great capstone, which lies beside the track that you follow down to the farm from the coastal path. If the pilgrim slept, the omens for recovery were good. If they were visited by a ravenous bird called Caladruis, they were not.

A church survived in the farmyard until the 1860s and is said to have contained the shrine of St Elvis, and an inscription recording that he baptised St David here. It was an important stopping place for medieval pilgrims en route to the city of St Davids. In the 19th century, the farmer did his best to

St Elvis Farm
Left: Barn built from the stone of the demolished church which contained the shrine of St Elvis.
Below: The cromlech.

ST ELVIS AND THE KING

St Elvis, whose name is a Latinised version of Eilfyw or Ailbhe, was bishop of Munster in Ireland. A cousin of St David, he lived from 454-528 and evangelised southern Ireland. He is in the tradition of Celtic or desert saints who roamed the land, establishing churches close to ancient pagan stones such as the one at St Elvis. The cromlech alongside St Elvis Farm was a double burial chamber with capstones measuring 3.5m (12ft) across, and St Elvis also established a monastery alongside it.

There is no other church dedicated to St Elvis in the UK, but there is a rather famous singer who was named after him. Fanciful though it may seem, the Cardiff academic Terry Breverton postulates a connection between the King and the Saint. In his book *A Welsh A-Z* he suggests that the Presley family name evokes the Preseli Hills, an expanse of wild moorland, heath and grassland that lies to the north of St Elvis. The American Presleys all had Welsh Christian names, and the famous one bore the names of two Welsh saints: Elvis Aron.

destroy the burial chamber by blowing it up but succeeded merely in fracturing the great stones, which remain in situ.

From here, another path completes the loop back to Solva. It is worth peeping into St Aidan's church, just above the harbour. In the porch is a 6th century pillar known as Maen Dewi, or St David's Stone, with an early Christian ring-cross carved onto it. It was rescued from use as a farm gatepost at St Elvis in 1925 and could actually be prehistoric.

The path to St Non's
The clifftop walk west from Solva is a dramatic one: the sea a foaming, surging cauldron of surf; the cliffs glistening coal-black rock slabs slashed with red and purple; the wind whipping the headlands; the bays brief havens of calm with their huddled, grey-sand beaches.

You are taken on a rhythmic, exhilarating rollercoaster ride as you bounce from headland to bay to headland, finally being tipped out at the chapel and holy well at St Non's. Actually there are two chapels here. The first you reach is the more

Below, left: St Non's Chapel (1934). **Centre**: St David's Stone. **Right**: St Non's Holy Well.

recent, built in 1934 by Carmarthen solicitor Cecil Morgan-Griffiths, close to the ruins of the original 6th century chapel and designed to replicate it. He used stone from cottages built with material scavenged from coastal chapels and monasteries destroyed at the Reformation.

St Non is said to have been St David's mother, and he was born in a house close to the ruined chapel, which you reach by first passing down a hedge-sheltered stone path to St Non's Holy Well – garlanded with daffodils when I visit in March – where the waters trickle from a shrine to the saint. Well and chapel have been venerated for 1400 years, and excavation at the chapel, built within a prehistoric stone circle, uncovered graves from the 7th century.

Above: The lifeboat station at St Justinian's.
Below: Approaching St David's Head.

St Non's to St Justinian's

Pressing on, the coast-path drama continues, over cliffs where the strata have been forced upright in great black quiffs of rock that are slicked with seaspray like Brylcreme. You dip down to Porthclais, the old harbour for St Davids, where the soggy moss on the rock face drips water like a great sage-green sponge being squeezed out, and then swing slowly round to the lifeboat house at St Justinian's. Here are St Justinian's chapel and well, a place of pilgrimage for medieval travellers to St Davids, now a ruin fenced off behind 'pri-

vate' signs in the garden of a bungalow. Justinian was a friend of St David, and became a hermit on nearby Ramsey Island. When he died, he was buried where his chapel now stands.

St David's Head

The landscape changes after St Justinian's, with sandy beaches in the bays at Porthselau and Whitesands (Porth Mawr in Welsh), the path running along behind them. I ease off my boots and take a paddle at Whitesands, the breakers getting me rather wetter than I had planned.

I was glad I had rested, for after Whitesands Bay comes another dramatic change in the landscape, as you ascend to St David's Head, where things get wild and rocky, and the path peters out as you traverse a boulder field. There are fine views back over Whitesands Bay and Ramsey Sound, which separates Ramsey Island from the mainland. The Irish and Celtic

Above: There's an excellent sandy beach at Whitesands Bay (Porth Mawr).

seas meet off the headland in a clashing of currents. In 140AD a Roman survey described St David's Head as the 'Promontory of the Eight Perils'.

One peril, for the walker, is losing your way, and I am concentrating on the map so intently that I almost miss the remains of a Neolithic burial chamber that is more intact than the one at St Elvis Farm. Measuring 6 metres by 2.5 metres, the massive capstone of Coetan Arthur (or Arthur's Quoit) is propped up at one end by a vertical stone. The 3000-year-old chamber, which is just to the right of the Pembrokeshire Coastal Path as you bear right around the headland, is one of many associated in folklore with King Arthur. He is said to have created the chamber by picking up and hurling the rocks to this spot.

I turn inland for the final approach to St Davids. The city sits in the middle distance, like the hub of a wheel of which the route of this walk is the misshapen rim. Almost all the route I have walked is laid out before me in a land-map of this remarkable pilgrimage. The lane that takes me into St Davids is an overlooked one – nothing passes me as I descend, coming right to the door of the cathedral.

St David's Cathedral

Unlike most cathedral cities, where the great church towers over the town, St David's is hunkered in a valley, beside the River Alun. It feels monastic here still. Alongside the church, cloistered in this green bowl, are the ruined bishop's palace and the intact refectory, the town barely visible up beyond the surviving cathedral gateway.

The church, with a banner welcoming pilgrims at the door, is built from the softer shades of stone I have admired on my walk: dark greys, lilac and purple. Inside, this stone is complemented by the time-bleached oak of the elaborate nave ceiling (**photo right**) and the choir stalls. It is a gentle uphill climb over the unique sloping floor to the shrine, which is tucked beyond the choir and close to the high altar.

The shrine, beautifully restored in 2012, bears icons of five saints, including St David and St Non. In a basket, notepaper bearing a scallop shell invites pilgrims to

ST DAVID

St David – *Dewi Sant* in Welsh – was a 6th century bishop of Mynyw, now St Davids. His shrine became a major draw in medieval times, when two pilgrimages here equalled one to Rome. The cathedral is built on the site of his 6th century monastery in the Glyn Rhosyn valley, and is the holiest site in Wales. His monastic rule was tough: monks ate only bread and vegetables – David's symbol, which became that of Wales, is the leek – and drank only water. They were forbidden oxen and pulled the plough themselves. David and his followers spread the faith throughout Wales and Brittany, and he became a saint in 1120. He is portrayed in both statue and icon in the cathedral with his emblem, a white dove. In his final sermon he is said to have urged the congregation: 'Do ye the little things in life'.

After Viking raiders removed his shrine, a new one was built in the 12th century, and the relics of St David – and St Justinian, who was also venerated here – were housed in a portable casket placed on the stone base. The shrine was again destroyed at the Reformation, its jewels stripped and the relics confiscated. However, the base remained, and forms the foundation of the restored shrine you see today.

record their prayer requests.

When I return for Evensong the daylight has faded, and the cathedral has undergone a subtle transformation. Now lit from within, the gold on the mosaics behind the high altar has come alive, spinning threads of golden

Croeso, Bererin i Dyddewi

Welcome, Pilgrim to St Davids

light that fill the space. Then come the soaring voices of the choir, and an organ that can scale the heights and plumb the depths, setting up a reverberation that sets your body buzzing in spiritual harmony.

Below: St David's Shrine.

9

A Thames pilgrimage

Dorchester-on-Thames to Abingdon, Oxford & Binsey

Four saints, a sacred river, and the shrine and holy well where Catherine of Aragon came to pray for a son

I had chanced upon a couple of cold, crisp, January days for my Thames pilgrimage. Days when the watery winter sun shines obliquely on a landscape powdered with frost, sending your long, slim shadow striding on ahead of you. Days when the chill air kept the water-meadow mud firm enough to support my size nines, and I could keep up a pace swift enough to work off the torpor brought on by Christmas and New Year over-indulgence.

The Thames is one of the stars of this pilgrimage, and at Dorchester you are plunged immediately into a spot where water has had a profound spiritual and religious significance for 6000 years. Dorchester Abbey is cradled to the south and west by the River Thames, and to the east by its little sister, the Thame. The two rivers, along with the flooded former gravel pits to the north, make this virtually an island.

The Thames at Abingdon

PRACTICAL INFORMATION

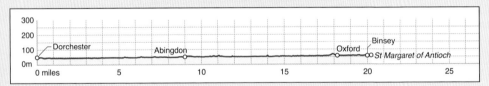

- **Terrain** The well-maintained Thames Path can be muddy in winter
- **Difficulty** Easy
- **Directions & GPS*** 009.pdf, 009.gpx, 009.kml at 🖳 https://trailblazer-guides.com/press

* See p10-11 for more information on downloads

ROUTE OVERVIEW   20.6 miles (33.2km)

Following the route of the Thames almost all the way means very little map-reading and plenty of time to just enjoy the walking, away from the usual busy approaches to-wards the 'dreaming spires' of Oxford.

Dorchester to Abingdon   9.2 miles (14.9km)

- **Time** 3hrs 15mins actual walking time
- **Total ascent** 170m/556ft
- **Map** OS Explorer *170 Vale of White Horse*

From Dorchester the route picks up the Thames Path, very well waymarked with its acorn signs, and follows it all the way to Abingdon. Being a riverside walk, the route is almost com-pletely flat, and passes Clifton Hampden **(3.5 miles)** and Culham Lock **(3.3 miles)**, reach-ing Abingdon in a further **2.4 miles**.

Abingdon to Oxford and Binsey   11.4 miles (18.3km)

- **Time** 3hrs 50mins actual walking time
- **Total ascent** 209m/685ft
- **Map** OS Explorer *170 Vale of White Horse; 180 Oxford*

You follow the Thames Path again today, walking via Sandford Lock **(5.3 miles)** and If-fley Lock **(1.7 miles)**, reaching Christ Church, Oxford in a further **1.7 miles**. The route leaves the Thames Path as you go through the city, but picks it up again when you return to the riverbank on the other side of town, finally leaving it at Fiddler's Island, in a fur-ther **1.8 miles**, for the last **0.9 mile** across meadows to Binsey.

Day walk options

- **By public transport** To reach Dorchester-on-Thames, take a train to Didcot Parkway then a bus or taxi. For Abingdon, travel by bus or taxi from either Didcot Parkway or Oxford.
- **Taxi option** Parkway Taxis (☎ 01235-603016, 🖳 pwtdidcot.co.uk)

Where to eat or stay along the way

● **Dorchester on Thames** Stay in *The George* (☎ 01865-340404, 🖥 historicinnz.co .uk/dorchester-on-thames, High St), built in 1495 and one of the oldest coaching inns in the country. Pack a **picnic lunch** from the Co-op (☎ 01865-340038, 43 High St; 7am-9pm) and eat it on the riverbank.

● **Clifton Hampden** If not picnicking, stop off for a **pub lunch** at the *Barley Mow* (☎ 01865-407847, 🖥 chefandbrewer.com; food daily noon-9pm, Clifton Hampden Bridge).

● **Abingdon** Stay at the perfect pilgrim resting place of *St Ethelwold's House* (☎ 01235-555486, 🖥 ethelwoldhouse.com, 30 East St Helen Street), a spiritual centre and B&B on the banks of the Thames. There is a wide choice of places to **eat** in the town.

● **Between Abingdon & Oxford** Enjoy a pub **lunch** by the Thames at either *The King's Arms*, **Sandford Lock** (☎ 01865-777095, 🖥 chefandbrewer.com; food noon-9pm) or the *Isis Farmhouse*, **Iffley Lock**

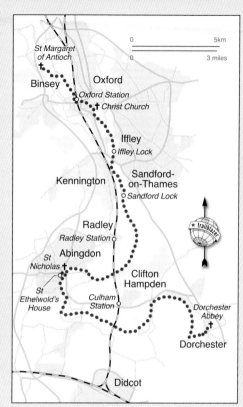

(☎ 01865-243854, 🖥 theisisfarmhouse.co.uk; food noon-9pm, closed Tue).

● **Oxford** Very wide selection of places to stay and eat.

PILGRIMAGE HIGHLIGHTS

● Visit **Dorchester Abbey** (🖥 dorchester-abbey.org.uk. open 8am-6pm, to dusk in winter) with its tomb of St Birinus, the Jesse Tree window and other treasures.
● Explore Abingdon's **Abbey Gardens** and surviving monastery outbuildings.
● Visit the shrine of St Frideswide at **Christ Church Oxford** (🖥 chch.ox.ac .uk/plan-your-visit; advance booking required).
● Complete your pilgrimage at the **Holy Well, St Margaret of Antioch** (🖥 osney benefice.org.uk/church/st-margaret-antioch-binsey) in Binsey.

Saints' feast days: St Ethelwold 1 August;
St Birinus 4 September CofE, 3 December Roman Catholic;
St Edmund 16 October; St Frideswide, 19 October (Oxford pilgrimage held close to it).

Dorchester Abbey

When St Birinus was sent from Rome in the 630s to convert Cynegils, King of Wessex, to Christianity, he baptised him in the Thame, which runs alongside the abbey. The two Saxon cathedrals and medieval monastic abbey that have in turn occupied this site give it a 1400-year tradition of Christian worship, and have bequeathed a very large parish church to this little village: the Abbey Church of St Peter and St Paul. Birinus was Dorchester's first bishop and his significance – and the bribes handed out to pilgrims (40 days off your time in purgatory, anyone?) – made this an important place of veneration in the Middle Ages.

The shrine built to hold Birinus's relics was destroyed at the Reformation, but most of the intricately carved vaulting was discovered in a blocked-up doorway in the 1870s and, in 1964, a replacement was made, incorporating the painted alcoves and blue vaulted upper section of the medieval shrine.

Other treasures include the lead font that survives from the 12th century monastery built on the site of the original Saxon cathedral, dedicated to St Birinus, in 635, and the window in the chancel depicting the Jesse Tree. This 14th century combination of tracery, sculpture and stained glass serves as Christ's *Who Do You Think You Are?* It depicts, generation by generation, his descent from King David's ancestor Jesse. Jesse himself lies recumbent in stone along the window sill, with his family sprouting out of him. At the top is Christ, his figure badly damaged by Cromwell's men, who must have been pretty determined at desecration to get that high.

Along the Thames to Abingdon

Walk the few hundred yards from abbey to Thames and you experience desecration from a more modern time, practised on a far more ancient sacred site. The unprepossessing grassy ridges you walk through

---

ST BIRINUS – DORCHESTER'S LOST AND FOUND SAINT

In the Middle Ages, every abbey wanted pilgrims, and to attract them it needed the relics of a saint that could be venerated. Dorchester had mislaid the remains of theirs, Birinus. The Venerable Bede said in 690 that Birinus's remains had been taken to Winchester Cathedral, but in 1224 someone conveniently remembered that, 50 years before, it had been revealed to an Augustinian Canon in a dream that Birinus's bits were in fact contained in a tomb in front of the altar. When the tomb was opened, visions and miracles occurred: a leper was cured, a dead man was brought back to life, and one canon became fluent in French in three days.

The recollection could not have been more timely. A few years before, Abbot Roger had bankrupted the abbey, grabbed the remaining cash and fled, seeking sanctuary at St Frideswide's Priory in Oxford. Now, Dorchester became a regional pilgrimage centre.

St Birinus's shrine, Dorchester Abbey

Dorchester Abbey

9

Above: River view, St Ethelwold's House.

are the remains of much higher ramparts, once part of a massive Iron Age fort. This is Dyke Hills, and it was ravaged by farm-ers in the 19th century. The ridges, known as *cursi*, were built in alignment with the river, and were used partly for ritual processions and ceremonies. They are evidence that the Thames was a sacred river to the ancient peoples of England; its name associated with the pre-Celtic idea of *tame* or *teme*, meaning darkness in the sense of holiness. Evidence has been uncovered of the ritualistic casting of swords and shields into the river.

Crossing via the weir to pick up the Thames Path, I see two sleek black cormorants, hunched on posts just where the water slows: fishy death foretold. From here the only map you need is the river itself, which leaves you free for contemplation as you pass through this restful, unchanging landscape.

ABINGDON'S TWO SAINTS – ST EDMUND AND ST ETHELWOLD

Abingdon boasts two saints. St Edmund of Abingdon was born in the town in 1175 and educated at the abbey. He was a priest and academic, lecturing in theology, dialectics and mathematics at the universities of Paris and Oxford and became Archbishop of Canterbury in 1233. He clashed with Henry III over the corruption of his court and in defence of the terms of Magna Carta, drawn up in 1215 to protect civil government, justice and the church. Edmund died in France in 1240 while on his way to make his case to the Pope.

The town's other saint, Ethelwold, was a Benedictine monk charged with reforming St Mary's Abbey in circa 960. Along with many other religious houses, it had fallen victim to corruption and abuse of power. Having established the Rule of St Benedict at St Mary's, under which celibate monks followed a life of physical work, contemplation, and seven religious offices (church services) a day, he was made Bishop of Winchester.

Ethelwold is remembered in Abingdon today through St Ethelwold's House in East St Helen Street, established in the 1960s by a school teacher called Dorothea Pickering. Since childhood, Dorothea had believed God had work for her to do in Abingdon, and knew that Ethelwold embodied the principles she admired. In 1967 she named her 800-year-old house in the saint's honour, created the Fellowship of St Ethelwold, and developed the house as an ecumenical spiritual centre. Dorothea died in 1997, but her vision has survived.

I have the riverbank pretty much to myself, apart from the herons stationed every few hundred yards but, near Culham Lock, I come across something new to me: a group of blackcaps, sleek little birds in morning-suit colours, fighting over the winter's dwindling stock of berries.

By the time the honeyed stone houses, former wharfs and surviving abbey buildings of Abingdon appear around a bend in the river I can feel the warmth of the winter sun on my back. When I arrive at St Ethelwold's House, the riverside garden is streaked sunset-pink and I take up the invitation to pop into one of the two summer houses that overlook the river, and rest my legs as I watch the boats glide by.

Above: Gateway to former Abingdon Abbey.
Below: Thames between Abingdon and Oxford.

Abingdon

Next morning, my first stop is St Nicolas church in the market place, where a tablet commemorates St Edmund of Abingdon. Beside the church, I pass under the gateway and on to the island where St Mary's Abbey stood. The few former domestic buildings that survive have been put to good use, with the timber-framed 13th century Checker Hall and bake house now housing the Unicorn Theatre. I take a peek into the impressive undercroft.

The walk from Abingdon to Oxford is another perfect stretch for contemplation, with the option of restorative stops at

Sandford Lock or Iffley Lock. For miles, I have the wide path through open country almost entirely to myself. I see few walkers, just a couple of boats chugging past: perfect conditions for talking things through with yourself.

Approaching by river, you really creep up on Oxford. One minute you are in open country then, immediately after your first glimpse of the dreaming spires, you pop up in St Aldate's, right in the heart of the city.

Christ Church Oxford, and St Frideswide

Most visitors to Christ Church come for the Harry Potter and Alice in Wonderland connections, rather than for St Frideswide. With that in mind, the tour route focuses on the Great Hall, the model for the one at Hogwarts, with its Alice window featuring Lewis Carroll (Charles Dodgson) and his heroine.

The pilgrim, however, will press on to the college chapel, which is also Oxford's cathedral, and stands on the site of the 8th century priory founded by St Frideswide. Her shrine, another jigsaw restoration job, stands in the

Top: First glimpse from the river of the spire of Christ Church Cathedral, Oxford.
Above: Statue of St Frideswide.

Above: The shrine of St Frideswide is in the cathedral with the stained glass window above it by Edward Burne-Jones.

Latin Chapel. Among the many pilgrims who came here was Catherine of Aragon – Henry VIII's first wife – who, in 1518, came to pray for the birth of a healthy son.

Above the shrine is St Frideswide's window, an early and uncharacteristic work by Christ Church alumnus Edward Burne-Jones, which tells her life in 16 panels. It sketches out her legend – a familiar one among female saints – of fleeing in the face of unwanted amorous advances, in her case from a Mercian prince, Algar. The final scene, of St Frideswide on her death bed has – curiously – a modern lavatory peeping out from behind a red curtain (see photo below).

Binsey and the Holy Well

St Frideswide fled from Oxford, and Algar, upriver to Binsey. I follow her, as did Catherine of Aragon, rejoining a Thames that is much diminished since I left it on the other side of town. Upstream of its confluence with the Cherwell it's only half the river it becomes south of the city. Cutting away from the river I reach the few houses that make up Binsey, where a very handy sign reading: 'The Perch' to the left and 'The Church' to the right points to all you need: a perfect country pub, and the 13th century St Margaret of Antioch, on the site where St Frideswide founded a second priory, and ended her days.

Algar's pursuit was halted at Binsey when he was struck blind by lightning, which Frideswide considered altogether too harsh. Her prayers to St Margaret, the pilgrim's favourite saint, brought forth a healing spring in the churchyard and the waters restored his sight. The spring then attracted pilgrims seeking a similar cure throughout the Middle Ages. The site was known as the Treacle Well: treacle in medieval times meaning 'healing unguent'. It was filled in at the Reformation, but a Victorian vicar restored it, and St Margaret's Well inspired the tale spun by the Dormouse in Lewis Carroll's *Alice's Adventures in Wonderland* of three little sisters named

Above: Entrance to St Margaret's Well, in the churchyard of Binsey church.
Below: The Thames north of Oxford.

Elsie, Lacie, and Tillie living in a well and surviving on treacle.

I step gingerly down the well steps and duck beneath a low canopy, where what looks rather like a washing-up bowl brims with dark, cool water. I dip my fingers in. On summer Sundays there is Evensong at this church: a perfect way to end this pilgrimage, with perhaps a pint at The Perch to follow.

10

London's saints and martyrs

From Westminster Abbey to Tyburn

A sacred-London pilgrimage in the footsteps of St Edward the Confessor and St Botolph, patron saint of travellers; touching the holy marks left by martyrs in the Tower of London; and visiting the greatest abbey and cathedral

To walk London as a pilgrim is to experience a very different city to the one a secular visitor encounters. To explore through the lives of saints and martyrs is to be drawn along by an undercurrent that most people miss. This is London as a city of both living and ancient faith and veneration.

PRACTICAL INFORMATION

- **Terrain** Generally flat pavements
- **Difficulty** Easy
- **Directions & GPS***
010.pdf, 010.gpx, 010.kml from
💻 https://trailblazer-guides.com/press
* See p10-11 for more information on downloads

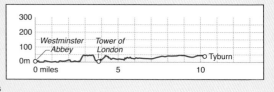

ROUTE OVERVIEW   9.9 miles (16km)

Although this walk itself is short and level, you have the option to climb steps to high points at several of the pilgrim destinations, affording wonderful city views.

It is easy to access almost any point on this walk by public transport and there is a huge choice of places to stay and eat.

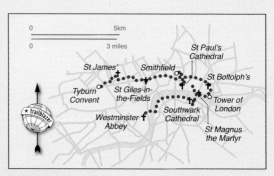

Westminster Abbey to the Tower of London   3.7 miles (6km)

- **Time** 1hr 30mins actual walking time
- **Total ascent** negligible
- **Map** OS Explorer *173 London North*

From Westminster Abbey you cross the Thames and then follow the Thames Path downriver to reach Winchester Palace in **1.9 miles** before leaving the river for Southwark Cathedral **(0.1 mile)** and The George inn **(0.1 mile)**. Then it is over London Bridge for the London Mithraeum and St Stephen Walbrook **(0.8 mile)** before heading downriver on the north bank, and the Thames Path, via St Magnus Martyr church **(0.4 mile)** to the Tower of London, reached after a further **0.4 mile**.

Tower of London to Tyburn Convent   6.2 miles (10km)

- **Time** 2hrs 15mins actual walking time
- **Total ascent** negligible
- **Map** OS Explorer *173 London North*

From the Tower of London the route follows the line of the old Roman city wall, going via St Botolph Aldgate **(0.5 mile)**, St Botolph Bishopsgate **(0.3 mile)** and St Botolph Aldersgate **(0.7 mile)** to reach St Paul's Cathedral after a further **0.4 mile**. From here the route continues east via St Bartholomew the Great church, at Spitalfields **(0.4 mile)**, and the Charterhouse **(0.2 mile)** to St Giles-in-the-Fields **(1.6 miles)** and St James Spanish Place **(1.2 miles)** to the site of the Tyburn Tree Gallows and the present-day Tyburn Convent, reached in a further **0.9 mile**.

Day walk options

The entire route can be completed in a day, provided you don't spend too long at each pilgrim point along the way.
- **One-day itinerary** Westminster Underground station (District & Circle line) is nearest to the start and Marble Arch (Central line) to the end.
- **Two-day itinerary** Use the London Underground network to access any point along the walk. The Underground station nearest to the mid-point at the Tower of London is Tower Hill (District & Circle line).

Where to eat or stay along the way

- **South Bank** Have **brunch** at one of the many Thames-side food trucks at the **South Bank Centre** (🖥 southbankcentre.co.uk/visit/cafes-restaurants-bars/scfood-market; Fri noon-8pm, Sat 11am-8pm, Sun noon-6pm).
- **Borough High St** Pause for a **drink** at *The George* (☎ 0207-407 2056, 11am-midnight, 75-77 Borough High St, SE1 1NH), a galleried inn that is as close as you can get to the one Chaucer's Canterbury pilgrims used.
- **Bedford Place** Stay at *The Penn Club* (☎ 0207-636 4718, 🖥 pennclub.co.uk, 21-23 Bedford Place WC1B 5JJ), a central-London Quaker-run club open to non-members for B&B.
- **St Giles High St** Eat **lunch** at *The Angel* (☎ 0207-240 2876, noon-10pm, 61 St Giles High St, WC2H 8LE), the pub where the condemned en route to the gallows at Tyburn were given a final drink.

PILGRIMAGE HIGHLIGHTS

- Set off on the right foot with a service at **Westminster Abbey** (🖥 westminster-abbey.org to check service times or book tickets to visit).
- Visit the **Tower of London** (🖥 hrp.org.uk/tower-of-london; 10am-6pm, EC3N 4AB) to see the holy marks cut into the walls by those about to be martyred, and the burial place of two murdered saints, two queens and Thomas Cromwell.
- Follow **St Botolph**, the patron saint of travellers, via three dedicated churches, and through a quiet Sunday-morning city.
- Take in a Sunday **service** or **recital** at **St Paul's Cathedral** (🖥 stpauls.co.uk, EC4M 8AD, see website for service times) and see the **Martyrs** video installation, or take a tour (Mon-Sat, check website for details), including climbing to the **Whispering Gallery**, or way up to the roof for a spectacular view.
- End your pilgrimage at the Shrine of the Martyrs at **Tyburn Convent** (🖥 tyburnconvent.org.uk/martyrs-shrine; guided tours usually 3.30pm but check in advance, 8-9 Hyde Park Pl) where public monastic afternoons are held on the first Sunday of the month.

Saints' feast days: St Edward the Confessor, 13 October. Westminster Abbey celebrates Edwardtide on the Saturday closest to this date.
St Botolph, 17 June in England, 25 June in Scotland.

10

Westminster Abbey

Ancient and modern stand side-by-side in Westminster Abbey. Above the north door are statues to ten modern martyrs (**photo above**). In niches left empty since the Reformation there are now 20th century victims of Nazism, communism and religious and racial prejudice, including Martin Luther King. Go inside and you find the shrine of a medieval saint: Edward the Confessor.

His tomb is beyond the Coronation Chair, glimpsed through a protective encirclement of the tombs of kings, reached

ST EDWARD THE CONFESSOR

Edward the Confessor, who re-founded Westminster Abbey in the 11th century, was the last Saxon king of England, reigning from 1042 until 1066. He was buried in the abbey and claims of miraculous cures at his tomb soon began. In 1130 Osbert of Clare, prior of Westminster, wrote a life of Edward in which he presented him as a holy man who could heal skin conditions through his touch, launching a belief in the healing power of monarchs that persisted until George I's time. He was canonised in 1161.

The title Confessor was bestowed on Edward because he was seen as being so devout and engrossed in the spiritual life that he could not engage with the material world, and because he did not achieve canonisation through martyrdom. His lack of heirs was assumed to be due to celibacy.

When Henry III rebuilt the abbey, in 1245, he created the grand new tomb for Edward that we see today. He was one of England's three patron saints until Edward III replaced them with the more war-like St George, in about 1350.

up a little wooden staircase that vaults the ramparts of departed royalty and takes you into St Edward's Chapel, and his sanctuary.

Except that for most visitors, for most of the time, it doesn't. A blue rope bars the way to an area too delicate to withstand the masses who throng the abbey. To reach the inner sanctum, you must book a verger-guided tour (see p123) or come on St Edward's day of National Pilgrimage: the Saturday closest to 13th October.

There is no greater church than Westminster Abbey. It has seen the coronation of every monarch since William the Conqueror and is the resting place of 3000 of the greatest individuals this nation has produced. In a chapel to one side of St Edward's shrine rest Elizabeth I and her half-sister Mary I, deadly rivals in life but united in death. A plaque urges us to 'remember before God all those who, divided at the Reformation by different convictions, laid down their lives for Christ and conscience sake.'

You depart not through the giftshop, as at Canterbury Cathedral, but through the wonderful cloister, a reminder that this was once a Benedictine monastery. Take the side passage to the Little Cloister and you find a secluded garden (**photo, left**) where a fountain tumbles: a precious place of peace in the heart of London, with a view of the Victoria Tower in the Palace of Westminster.

They sell pilgrim badges which, they explain, were invented to persuade pilgrims not to chip pieces off the shrine. I get a silver roundel bearing St Edward's face for a modest £3.95.

Southwark

From here I follow the south bank of the Thames, past secular draws such as the London Eye, the South Bank complex, and Shakespeare's Globe. The views down-river combine God and Mammon in one frame: St Paul's Cathedral, the 'Walkie Talkie', the 'Cheesegrater' and a cluster of lesser carbuncles. Approaching Southwark, the way suddenly narrows to an approximation of old riverside London, with a sheer brick cliff of wharves to my left and, to my right, an unexpected piece of the medieval: the fenced-off surviving end wall of Winchester Palace, home to that city's powerful bishop. Southwark was the

Left: The remains of Winchester Palace. **Right and centre**: Southwark Cathedral and roof boss.

Above: The galleried George Inn.

Above: The London Mithraeum.

starting point for pilgrims headed to Canterbury, and the shrine of St Thomas Becket. Tucked in alongside Borough Market is Southwark Cathedral, an Augustinian priory before the Reformation.

In *The Canterbury Tales*, Chaucer's pilgrims refreshed themselves at The Tabard, just to the south of the cathedral. While the Tabard has gone, The George, a very similar galleried inn in the same square, gives the pilgrim a chance to echo them.

St Magnus and the London Mithraeum

Many of those pilgrims would have arrived from north of the Thames via the old London Bridge, at the centre of which stood a chapel dedicated to St Thomas. At the north end of the bridge is St Magnus Martyr, rebuilt by Sir Christopher Wren after the fire of London. I can just see it, dwarfed by modern office blocks, as I cross the river on the new bridge, but I suggest a slight diversion before visiting it. It involves a loop that takes in two very special places for the pilgrim interested in the

Below: The 1677 Monument.

diversity of buildings dedicated to the glory of God, or a god, within a few hundred metres of St Magnus.

The first is the London Mithraeum, also known as the Roman Temple of Mithras, now buried beneath the European headquarters of Bloomberg, but made accessible through a deal with the Museum of London. The cult of Mithras was a mysterious one, with rituals that sound a little like Freemasonry, but with rather more emphasis on the slaughter of bulls. You are promised an immersive, theatrical experience and enter in complete darkness; the temple gradually emerging from the gloom as the lights come up to the pulse of ominous music.

The second, just across the street, is St Stephen Walbrook, a Wren masterpiece and his own parish church, completed in 1672. I step into a grand dome, filled with windows and flooded with light, its centrepiece a great white-rock altar by Henry Moore. On the way back to St Magnus Martyr, I pass the

1677 Monument to the Fire of London and can't resist paying to pound up the 311 steps of this stone candlestick surmounted by a golden orb thrusting elegantly up among the lumpen modern buildings. The view is worth the climb, enabling you to pick out the spires of other Wren churches that once dominated the skyline, but are now dwarfed by modern buildings.

St Magnus Martyr is my favourite Wren church; an oasis of calm clutched in the noisome armpit formed by Lower Thames St and London Bridge. It stands where the old London Bridge reached the shore, and there is a wonderfully detailed scale model of that bridge in the church, as well as a pilgrim shrine to Our Lady of Walsingham. T S Eliot writes of the splendour of St Magnus's white and gold walls in *The Wasteland*.

Above: Stained glass window showing the old London Bridge, and Our Lady of Walsingham shrine in the church of St Magnus Martyr.

Martyrs' marks in the Tower of London

Following the Thames Path takes me to The Tower of London, where the Beef-

eaters bellow out tales of torture and dismemberment in a tone that suggests you shouldn't take such suffering too seriously. Come as a pilgrim, however, and those horrors are all too real. In the Salt Tower, where many martyrs were imprisoned, the stone walls are etched with their names and symbols of the Catholic faith they refused to renounce: holy marks that bear witness to terrible suffering.

Just west of the Salt Tower is Traitors' Gate, through which St Thomas More, Henry VIII's chancellor, was brought by boat from Westminster Hall, having been convicted of treason. More had refused to accept his king's divorce from Catherine of Aragon. When, in 1535, he left his cell in the Bell Tower and walked to his death on Tower Hill, he refused wine offered en route, saying: 'My Master, Christ, had vinegar and gall'. His remains lie in the Tower's Chapel Royal, in the north-

Left and below: Salt Tower at The Tower of London and graffiti left by Catholics who refused to renounce their faith.

10

west corner, along with those of other victims of Henry VIII including St John Fisher, Queen Anne Boleyn, Queen Katherine Howard and Thomas Cromwell.

Sunday in the city of St Botolph

Sunday is quiet in the City. The bankers are gone and it offers little for secular tourists. So you are at peace to touch on three churches dedicated to St Botolph, patron saint of travellers. Little is known of Botolph except that, in the 7th century, he established a monastery at Boston (Botolph's Town) in Lincolnshire. His remains were brought to Westminster Abbey, processing through four city gateways on their way: Billingsgate, Aldgate, Bishopsgate and Aldersgate. A church dedicated to him was built alongside each of these, and the last three survive.

So you can follow the curving line of the old city wall and take in St Botolph's at Aldgate, Bishopsgate and Aldersgate. In the 1370s Chaucer lived above Aldgate gatehouse and, in 1684,

St Botolph's Bishopsgate.

Above: A glimpse of St Paul's.

Daniel Defoe was married in this church. Each church is boxed in by office towers, but all have a park alongside them. The one at Aldersgate, Postman's Park, has within it the Watts Memorial to Heroic Self-Sacrifice. On a wall beneath a sheltering tiled roof are rather lovely ceramic plaques (**see photos below**) memorialising individuals who gave their lives to save others. One is to a passenger on a Thames steamboat who leapt overboard to save a child and was drowned; another to a railwayman who rescued a suicidal woman from the tracks at Woolwich Arsenal station but was himself killed by the train.

St Paul's Cathedral

To move from these simple memorials for forgotten heroes to the grandeur of nearby St Paul's is a jolt. On Sundays, when I suggest you visit, the cathedral is only open for worship, and you can best experience the power and majesty of this place, from the towering memorial to Wellington to the spectacular mosaic ceiling in the choir, and the

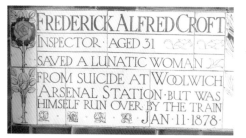

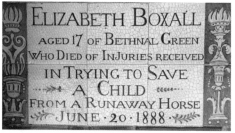

splendour of the high altar beneath the stately Baroque *baldacchino*, or canopy.

You may also be able to slip into the south transept to see *Martyrs (Earth, Air, Fire, Water)*, a video installation by Bill Viola and Kira Perov in which four individuals remain resolute beneath onslaughts including overpowering plumes of water and consuming flames. The explanation alongside says these figures 'exemplify the human capacity to bear pain, hardship and even death in order to remain faithful to their values, beliefs, and principles... [and that they represent] action, fortitude, perseverance, endurance, and sacrifice.'

Smithfield & the journey to martyrdom

Smithfield, my next focus, has a cluster of pilgrim points. Two great religious houses occupied land to either side of the present meat market, and significant parts have survived. To the north is the Charterhouse, a former Carthusian monastery which became a school and is now a rather special retirement home. I ask if you have to be an old Carthusian – monk or schoolboy – to qualify, but no, anyone can apply who is over 65, single, and without property. It looks a convivial life. They go to the pub at noon three days a week, do

Left: Magnificent choir ceiling, St Paul's. **Below**: View of Paternoster Square and the column from the dome of St Paul's.

Above: The priory church of
St Bartholomew the Great (St Bart's).

some work, pursue their own interests.

To the south is the former priory of St Bartholomew, which has now billowed into a great modern hospital, but where the Priory church of St Bartholomew the Great survives. It has the finest Norman church interior in London, according to John Betjeman. You may recognise it from the 1994 romantic comedy *Four Weddings and a Funeral*. Church and hospital were founded by Prior Rahere, who received the charter from Henry I in 1133.

As a plaque by his tomb beside the altar says: 'From the moment of its foundation his church attracted those who were sick and sought healing from God by the intercession of our patron saint, the Apostle Bartholomew. If you or someone you know is sick, light a candle here and ask for prayers of our patron and our founder, for God is wonderful in his saints'.

The next pilgrim point is at St Sepulchre, which stands almost opposite the Old Bailey, and the site of Newgate Gaol. On the day of an execution, the bells of St Sepulchre tolled as the condemned were hauled onto a hurdle, a rough sledge, and

Above: Inside St Bartholomew the Great – the 'finest Norman church interior in London', according to John Betjeman.

paraded through the streets to the gallows at Tyburn.

I follow their journey. When they reached St Giles-in-the-Fields, the last church before Tyburn, they were allowed a final drink at The Angel pub next door, in a tradition begun in the 15th century and known as St Giles's Bowl. It's where the phrase 'falling off the wagon' is said to have originated. There is still an Angel on the site. I push open the door and find a peaceful haven. This quiet local might not be my choice for a final drink, but it's perfectly acceptable for a pilgrim Sunday lunch.

St James of Compostela

From here, what is now Oxford Street would speed martyrs and common criminals

Above: Statue of St James the Great of Compostela in the pilgrim church of St James' Spanish Place.

to their deaths, but I take a diversion along Marylebone back streets to St James', Spanish Place, a pilgrim church *par excellence*. Dedicated to St James the Great of Compostela, it has a statue of him bearing his pilgrim scallop shell, plus a martyrs' chapel.

And then it is just another lope along the back streets to Marble Arch, and the site of the Tyburn gallows. Tyburn Convent, with its Martyrs' Shrine, has stood close by since 1901. It was founded by a community of Benedictine nuns that fled France to escape restrictions on religious orders, and with its altar to the martyrs it offers a reflective end to this London pilgrimage.

10

THE KING'S GALLOWS AT TYBURN

Tyburn was London's place of execution from 1196 until 1783, and an estimated 50,000 met their end here over six centuries, including 105 Roman Catholic Reformation martyrs.

Theirs was a protracted, painful end. Victims were first hanged at the gallows, but cut down before death, then 'drawn' – their entrails torn out – and finally beheaded and their bodies cut into quarters, the parts being displayed in public as a warning to others. Thomas Cromwell's body was brought here, after his decapitation at Tower Hill.

St John Houghton, prior of the Carthusian monastery at Charterhouse and the first Reformation martyr, was executed at Tyburn, as was St Edmund Campion, a Jesuit priest who conducted an underground ministry in England, hiding in priest holes in the houses of Catholics until being captured in 1581. He was canonised in 1970.

11

St Peter's Way

Purleigh to the Chapel of St Peter-on-the-Wall, Essex

Across the Essex marshes to the 1300-year-old chapel of St Peter-on-the-Wall, one of the oldest churches in England

Not always easy to love, the Essex marshes. For some they are too austere, too remote, too all-round flat and featureless. And, when a harsh north-easterly wind is whipping in off the North Sea, they can feel forsaken. Yet, for others, all of this just adds to their appeal.

St Cedd was among the latter. As a 7th century missionary, he sought out wild, remote places to plant the seeds of Celtic Christianity, and the site of a Roman fort way out on the tip of the marshes beyond Bradwell-on-Sea was perfect. The church he built, St Peter-on-the-Wall, has survived, and makes a powerfully stark and austere climax to a walk along St Peter's Way, which you follow throughout.

In contrast to the pilgrimages that end at cathedrals, my destination here is a sacred site that – materially – could not be more unassuming, but it is no less powerful for that, and the experience of walking there leaves room for contemplation as you absorb the far views over this low country.

Mundon Creek

PRACTICAL INFORMATION

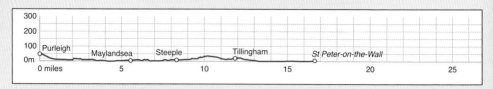

- **Terrain** Very flat, generally distinct paths over farmland. One short stretch after Steeple along busy road with no pavement.
- **Difficulty** Easy
- **Directions & GPS*** 011.pdf, 011.gpx, 011.kml at ⌨ https://trailblazer-guides.com/press

* See p10-11 for more information on downloads

ROUTE OVERVIEW   16.6 miles (26.7km)

This mainly level walk along St Peter's Way offers plenty of bird-spotting opportunities so you might want to take binoculars. Check the weather forecast before setting off and be prepared with the right clothing as the flat Essex marshes can experience harsh winds off the North Sea.

Purleigh to Steeple   8 miles (12.8km)

- **Time** 3 hours actual walking time   ● **Total ascent** 49m/160ft
- **Map** OS Explorer *176 Blackwater Estuary*

From Purleigh, follow St Peter's Way across flat fields for **3.2 miles** to Mundon, and then over the marshes and along the shore to Maylandsea in a further **1.9 miles**. Then it is back inland to Steeple, reached in a further **2.9 miles**.

Steeple to St Peter-on-the-Wall   8.6 miles (13.9km)

- **Time** 3hrs 15mins actual walking time   ● **Total ascent** 51m/168ft
- **Map** OS Explorer *176 Blackwater Estuary*

From Steeple, St Peter's Way rises gently but steadily over farmland, then drops down to reach Tillingham after **4 miles**. You then cross marshes to the seawall, which it follows north to the Chapel of St Peter-on-the-Wall, in **4.6 miles**. The nearest village to the chapel is Bradwell-on-Sea, just under 2 miles away.

Day walk options

For a little more of a challenge, this entire walk could be completed in one day. For a shorter walk, begin at Steeple.

- **By public transport** Take the train to Chelmsford, then a bus or taxi to begin the walk at Purleigh. If beginning at Steeple, the nearest station is Southminster. To return home from St Peter-on-the-Wall, walk to Bradwell-on-Sea for a bus to Southminster station, or a take a taxi directly from St Peter's.
- **Taxi option** Dengie Taxis (☎ 07496-609697, ⌨ dengietaxis.co.uk).

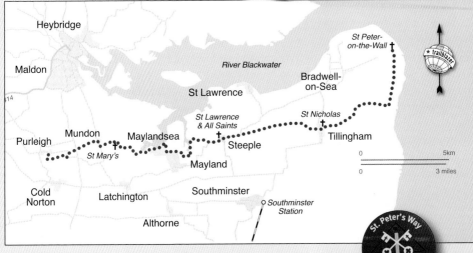

Where to eat or stay along the way

● **Steeple** Stay at the *Star Inn* (☎ 01621-772646, 🖳 the starinnsteeple.co.uk, The Street), a friendly village local with decent pub grub.

● **Maylandsea** is the perfect location for a picnic lunch.

● **Tillingham** Stop for **lunch** at the *Fox and Hounds* (☎ 01621-779416, 🖳 facebook.com/pages/Fox-Hounds) a lovely pub on the village green.

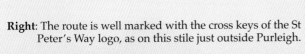

Right: The route is well marked with the cross keys of the St Peter's Way logo, as on this stile just outside Purleigh.

PILGRIMAGE HIGHLIGHTS

● The **'petrified' forest** and 14th century church of **St Mary's** at **Mundon** (🖳 friendsoffriendlesschurches.org.uk/mundon, 10am-4pm)

● Navigating the tidal creeks, mudflats and saltmarsh to **Maylandsea** and stopping to watch the boats and birds in the marina

● The walk across the wild marshes to **St Peter-on-the-Wall** where the **Othona Community** welcome pilgrims (🖳 othonaessex.org.uk; contact them for details)

Celebration day Bradwell Pilgrimage and Gathering, first Saturday in July
(🖳 bradwellpilgrimage.co.uk)

Purleigh

As I set off from the village of Purleigh, there is nothing harsh about the weather. Today is one of the bright ones that capricious May sometimes slips our way, even out here on the edge of the North Sea.

Purleigh sits on a modest rise, placing me on the lip of a shallow bowl that stretches far ahead, giving a panoramic view over Mundon to Maylandsea. The route, following a path re-established by the Ramblers' Association, is through rich arable land dotted with handsome 17th and 18th century farmhouses, evidence of just how fat farmers became here.

Mundon

The vast prairie-like fields are relieved at Mundon. Just

beyond the village, within the protective moat that once embraced a fortified Saxon manor house, is the 14th century timber-framed church of St Mary's. It has not been used for worship since the 1970s, but the Friends of Friendless churches piloted extensive renovation. It stands in a little clearing within a protective belt of woodland, and has been beautifully restored, the interior resonating with a subtle, sacred glow.

If you want evidence that these marshes can be stark and mysterious, Mundon provides it. Just past the church is an eerie array of dead oak and ash trees, the last remnants of an ancient forest. It's known as the 'petrified forest' although the wood is not actually petrified. The trees throw shapes at the grazing sheep,

Above: The timber-framed church of St Mary's, Mundon. **Opposite**: Mundon petrified forest.

which remain resolutely unspooked, but more impressionable people have put the plight of these trees down to witchcraft. I can't help spotting what looks like a face peering out from a gnarled wound where a bough has split away.

Maylandsea

Everything changes as you approach Maylandsea. Here I enter a network of tidal creeks, mudflats, shingle beaches and saltmarsh, the path winding along the top of the sea wall. In the distance I see the masts of many boats prickling the sky above the village marina, and the sound of many lanyards chiming in the wind like a percussion section enjoying an endless jam session.

Maylandsea was an oyster fishing area for a thousand years, and the links to seafaring remain. The path takes you through a working boatyard, and there are one or two traditional fishing smacks and Thames barges moored among the pleasure boats in the marina.

The Blackwater Estuary, just to the north of the path, is an important area for birds. Look out here, and tomorrow on the marshes beyond Tillingham, for abundant bird life including grey heron, oystercatcher and little egret. In autumn, terns, skuas and gannets abound, and in winter godwit, dunlin and plover, among many others.

Steeple

Then it's back inland to Steeple. True to its name, the steeple of St Lawrence and All Saints church is a marker on your winding approach to the village. But it's a modest little thing, just a finger raised. The village

Below: Maylandsea marina.
Left: On the marina walkway.

has a handy pub – The Star Inn – that also does B&B. This is the half-way point and marks a switch back to the landscape from the first stage of the walk.

Although you pass through farmland, this is a remote stretch, white bird-scaring windsocks fluttering above the fields, and a good place for contemplation. I take a rest on the edge of a wood. The may blossom is out in all its white-confetti glory, and being mobbed by bees, and I'm getting in exactly the right pilgrim frame of mind when a sound starts up that drags me back to the present. Somewhere in the bushes a bird I cannot see or identify is blasting out a top-volume cacophony of squawks, screeches and chirps that reminds me of a pinball machine racking up a massive bonus score. Then its mate chimes in with a sound like a jackpot payout from a one-armed bandit. I give up, deciding contemplation will have to wait until I reach the edge of the marsh.

Above: St Nicholas's Church, Tillingham.

The prairie fields are back and, once I've traversed a string of them, I begin to feel like a cartoon man crawling over the desert, tongue hanging out. So I'm very happy to reach Tillingham, its village green bookended by the Fox and Hounds pub and St Nicholas's church.

St Peter's Way has shunned the direct approach to St Peter-on-the-Wall, which would follow the route of the Roman road via Bradwell-on-Sea. Instead, you get this lovely loop through Tillingham, running

ST CEDD

Anglo-Saxon St Cedd was sent as a boy to the monastery at Lindisfarne, Northumberland (which features in Walk 19), to be educated and trained as a priest and missionary. He became a bishop and was sent first to bring Christianity to the people of Mercia, in the present-day Midlands. He was so successful there that King Sigbert of the East Saxons asked for a similar mission in his kingdom of present-day Essex.

In 653 Cedd sailed down the east coast from Lindisfarne, landing at Bradwell, where he established his mission. Here, on the sea wall, he built a church, hospital, library, school, farm and guest house and created a community of men and women who could take the Christian story throughout Sigbert's kingdom. That church, St Peter-on-the-Wall, still stands today.

In 659, Cedd returned to Northumbria, where he established another monastery at Lastingham. When he was struck down by the plague five years later, it is said that 30 monks from Bradwell travelled to pray at his bedside, but to no avail. All died alongside St Cedd, apart from one young boy who returned to Bradwell with the grim news.

right through the churchyard at St Nicholas, before heading out to the sea and then swinging north for the final approach.

St Peter-on-the-Wall

St Peter's is there in the distance, a gradually enlarging ragstone lozenge on the horizon, for the last couple of miles. It is

Above: The chapel of St Peter-on-the-Wall was built by St Cedd in the 7th century. In parts of the walls Roman bricks (**inset**) were reused.

Above: Looking out to sea from St Peter's.

such a simple, modest, yet remarkable building. The very fact of its survival since the 7th century is a triumph. After the Norman Conquest this became a Benedictine monastery but failed to prosper and was sold for secular use in 1371. For centuries the church was reduced to a barn in which grain was stored and cattle sheltered. The marks of its many life-stages are evident in the walls, from the lines of Roman brick to the filled-in arches that once allowed carts to rumble in.

I step inside and find a simple space: rough-stone walls, a flagstone floor, sturdy wooden bench pews and a simple cross high on the wall behind the altar. Nothing grand, nothing to take your breath away, yet all the more affecting for that. It is a blank canvas, the perfect apex of a very personal pilgrimage.

ST PETER'S RESTORED: THE OTHONA COMMUNITY

In 1920 St Peter's was restored as a chapel and, in 1946, was discovered by an Anglican clergyman, Norman Motley. Motley had been seeking a place in which to rekindle the comradeship he had experienced during World War II, when social and religious barriers lost their relevance. He established the non-denominational Othona Community here, naming it after the Roman fort that stood on the site. The community grew into a national network and established a retreat. Its pilgrim complex stands just north of the chapel, of which they say: 'The chapel connects us to the Celtic Christian past. This means honouring nature and all of the cosmos, which is written into Othona's DNA'

12

St Edmund's Way

Thetford to Bury St Edmunds

Through a royal forest and along the River Lark on the trail of a bereaved king and a murdered saint

Even on a day like this, under a perfect, cobalt blue sky, Thetford's ruined priory can look like just another pile of stones. But these fractured walls are also the bones of a remarkable story.

Henry VIII hovers as a ghostly spectre over all the shrines that he destroyed, but his presence here, at the riverside Priory of Our Lady of Thetford, is stronger than at any other. This was one of the last of the monasteries Henry seized, and for one very good reason: it contained the tomb of his illegitimate son, Henry FitzRoy, who died of consumption at the age of 17.

Another king haunts the destination of this pilgrimage. The shrine of the Anglo-Saxon martyr-king St Edmund, killed by the Danes in 869, stood in the very similar riverside grounds of a now-ruined abbey in Bury St Edmunds.

Both were popular places of pilgrimage in the Middle Ages, and the walk between them through the ancient King's Forest and along the River Lark borrows from two long distance paths, the Icknield Way and St Edmund's Way, to create a truly magical pilgrimage.

The ruins of Thetford Priory

PRACTICAL INFORMATION

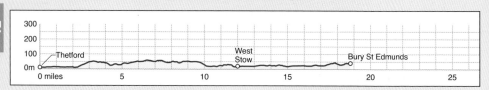

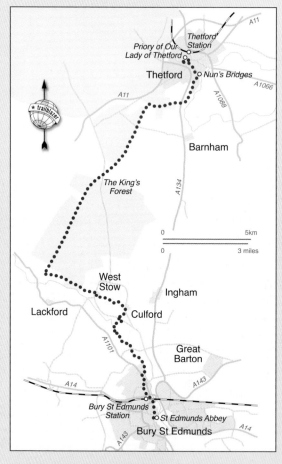

- **Terrain** Mainly forest tracks and riverside paths, with some town pavements.
- **Difficulty** Easy
- **Directions & GPS***
012.pdf, 012.gpx, 012.kml from https://trailblazer-guides.com/press
  * See p10-11 for more information on downloads

ROUTE OVERVIEW
18.9 miles (30.4km)

A gentle, peaceful walk through woodland and along riverbanks, bookended by thought-provoking ruins. Although you are on St Edmund's Way throughout the walk, signage is inconsistent and of limited help. Make sure you have lunch and plenty of water with you on the first day as there are no hostelries en route.

Thetford to West Stow   11.9 miles (19.2km)

- **Time** 4hrs 20mins actual walking time ● **Total ascent** 148m/485ft
- **Map** OS Explorer 229 *Thetford Forest in the Brecks*

Walk out of Thetford along the banks of the Little Ouse for **1.2 miles**, then across Barnham Cross Common to reach the King's Forest in **1.1 miles**. You walk through the forest for **8 miles** before taking a quiet lane into West Stow, reached in a further **1.6 miles**. The route is flat all the way to Bury St Edmunds.

West Stow to Bury St Edmunds
7 milcs (11.2km)

- **Time** 2hrs actual walking time
- **Total ascent** 45m/147ft
- **Map** OS Explorer *229 Thetford Forest in the Brecks; 211 Bury St Edmunds & Stowmarket*

Another waterside stretch to begin with, alongside an elongated lake for **1.4 miles** to Culford Park, then another **1.4 miles** across flat country to reach the River Lark. You follow the river for **2.7 miles** to the outskirts of Bury St Edmunds, and reach your destination in **1.5 miles**.

Day walk options

For a vigorous walk, complete the entire route in one day. For a shorter walk, begin at West Stow.

- **By public transport** Take the train to Thetford station to begin the walk, and from Bury St Edmunds station at the end. If beginning at West Stow, take a bus or taxi from Bury St Edmunds station.
- **Taxi option** Perry's Taxis (☎ 07985-386059 or ☎ 01842-769686; 🖥 perrystaxis.co.uk)

Where to eat or stay along the way

- **Thetford** Stay at *The Bell Hotel,* (☎ 01842 754455, 🖥 greenekinginns.co.uk, King St) an old coaching inn at the centre of this ancient market town.
- **West Stow** Stay at *West Stow Hall* (☎ 01284 728127, 🖥 weststowhall.com, Icklingham Rd) or try glamping at *West Stow Pods* (☎ 01284 728136, 🖥 weststowpods.co.uk).
- **Bury St Edmunds** Eat in **Abbey Gardens** (8am-5pm) at the *Pilgrim's Kitchen* (☎ 01284 748738; Mon-Sat 9am-4pm, Sun 10am-3pm) for great lunches, or enjoy alfresco coffee and cake from *Abbey Gardens Café* (☎ 01284 758380).

PILGRIMAGE HIGHLIGHTS

- Explore the ruins of **Thetford Priory** (🖥 english-heritage.org.uk/visit/places/thetford-priory, Water Ln; 9am-4pm), once the burial place of Henry VIII's illegitimate son.
- Enjoy the peace of walking in the **King's Forest** and along the banks of the **River Lark**.
- Visit **Bury St Edmunds Abbey** (☎ 01284-757490, 🖥 english-heritage.org.uk, Angel Hill; 9am-5pm), **St Edmundsbury Cathedral** (🖥 stedscathedral.org, Angel Hill) and **St Mary's** (🖥 wearechurch.net, Honey Hill), burial place of Henry VIII's sister, Mary Tudor.

12

Thetford

Today, Thetford is famed more for its connection with the classic BBC comedy *Dad's Army*. Many location sequences were filmed here, in this sleepy market town. There is a museum dedicated to the show, and I pass a bronze statue of Captain Mainwaring sitting on a bench as I take the riverside path, by a peaceful, tree-lined, water highway that flows right through town.

An altogether more remarkable story brought pilgrims here in the Middle Ages: a statue of the Virgin Mary, which was said to perform miracles. According to a 15th century account, Mary appeared three times in the dreams of a Thetford artisan suffering from an incurable complaint. She told him he would be restored to health if he could persuade the prior to build a Lady Chapel in stone beside his church. The prior began to build, but only in wood. Then came a remarkable discovery: a long-forgotten wooden statue of the Virgin. It was found that a hollow carved into its head contained some remarkable relics, with identifying descriptions engraved on lead wrappings. Among them were, reputedly, a relic from Jesus's robe, another from his manger, a third from Mary's girdle, plus the relics of a whole list of saints. Top trumps!

A letter with the remains said that they had been sent from the Church of the Holy Sepulchre in Jerusalem at the request of Hugh Bigod, founder of Thetford's priory. A series of miraculous cures followed the discovery, and the pilgrims' offerings enabled the abbot to revise his building plans, creating a Lady Chapel in stone.

There are other reminders of Thetford's appeal for pilgrims. Just across the Little Ouse river from the priory are the sole surviving remains in England of a priory of the canons of the Holy Sepulchre, who aided medieval pilgrims on their way to Jerusalem. The church became a barn and, in the 19th century, the ruins were adapted as an ornamental garden grotto.

Through the King's Forest

There is a further monastery site at Nuns' Bridges, which the path crosses as it weaves on and off islands in the stream,

THETFORD PRIORY AND A PLEA TO HENRY VIII

The 12th century Priory of Our Lady of Thetford was one of the largest and most important monasteries in medieval East Anglia and was the burial place of the Earls and Dukes of Norfolk for 400 years. The body of Henry FitzRoy, Duke of Richmond, was brought here because he had been married to Norfolk's daughter, Mary Howard, and Henry VIII entrusted the funeral arrangements to Norfolk. Born to Henry's mistress, Elizabeth Blount, during his marriage to Catherine of Aragon, Richmond was the only illegitimate son acknowledged by Henry. For a time, the king even planned to name Richmond his heir, despite his illegitimacy.

The Duke of Norfolk hoped Richmond's presence in his family tomb at the priory would sway Henry when he petitioned to have this monastery spared. Its suppression was delayed by four years, but in 1540 it went the way of every other monastic house. The Howard family tomb was moved to St Michael's Church, Framlingham, and Richmond's body with it.

Through the King's Forest

12

before I walk over Barnham Cross Common and reach the woods that will lead me to the King's Forest.

As I swap rough heathland for woodland, and the noise of road and town fade, it is like entering a hushed cloister. As my eyes adjust to the sudden darkness, what I first think is a fox slinks out into the path ahead of me. But it's not a fox, it's a miniature deer, a muntjac. And, once it senses me, it's off.

Woodland walks can be oppressive, but the King's Forest is not just a blanket of conifers shutting out the light, it also has blocks of heath, and fields, and the path follows a soft, sandy track that is very easy on the feet. The sand underfoot adds to the muffled silence of the woods, and to the sense of being cloistered in nature.

My silent passage fools another muntjac, which does a comedy screech to a halt as it rounds a bend and discovers me. Its ears prick up, it thinks for a second, then flits off into the trees. There are to be several more encounters that startle the wildlife. I inadvertently creep up on a pheasant, dozing in a dip beside the path. It rises right in front of me and flies off with a squawk. Then there is the squadron of swallows, zooming in like little Spitfires, tumbling in aerial combat. At the last second they spot me and, with a flick of the wings, peel off to left or right. I hear a rustling in the undergrowth right beside me, and peer in to see if this is another muntjac. In fact it's just a blackbird sorting through the dried leaves like someone dealing with their laundry. Evidently the blackbird is about to do a brown wash.

I'm so intent on watching for wildlife in the woods to my right that I don't notice, in the potato field to my left, an irrigation system is arcing a great sheet of water my way. So I get a sudden cold shower or, as I prefer to think of it as a pilgrim, an unexpected supplementary baptism.

West Stow, Culford & along the River Lark

The solitude has been so complete in the forest that walking along a road to West Stow takes a bit of getting used to, but this short stretch of the walk offers a place to pause before the next day's riverside walk to Bury St Edmunds.

West Stow Hall, a suggested overnight stay, is a lovely Tudor house with connections to Mary Tudor, Henry VIII's sister,

Above: West Stow Hall.
Right: Culford Hall.
Below: The walk passes Culford Lake.

who we shall encounter again at Bury St Edmunds. You'll see the house off to your left as you approach the village. It's a magnificent place, built in 1520 by Mary's Master of the Horse, Sir John Crofts, and has a truly imposing red brick gatehouse.

You pass St Mary, West Stow, a much-altered church with a Norman heart, and many 14th century features, before entering Culford Park, landscaped by Humphrey Repton in the 18th century. A stretch along the banks of its reed-fringed, elongated lake brings you past the grand mansion of Culford Hall, now a school. Once all this belonged to the abbey at Bury

12

St Edmunds. Tucked around the corner after you pass the house is the Victorian church of St Mary, Culford, shaded by majestic pines.

A little tacking across country brings me to the River Lark, which will now be my faithful guide much of the way to Bury St Edmunds. Alongside the splendidly named Ducksluice Farm a cuckoo, brazen con merchant, makes its persistent call. Across the fields to my left is the tower of a ruined church in an abandoned village, and then it is just a trek along the fringe of a golf course before I reach the suburbs of Bury St Edmunds.

Bury St Edmunds

The first sight of St Edmundsbury cathedral towering above the trees and the medieval houses on Angel Hill might suggest that this is one abbey church that survived the Reformation. In fact, it didn't. After you pass through the magnificent Abbey Gateway and into the abbey's 14-acre riverside garden, you see the sparse remains of the original abbey church beyond the current cathedral.

The present St Edmundsbury Cathedral owes its existence to a failed pilgrimage to Compostela. In the 12th century, Abbot Anselm was unable to complete the Way of St James so instead he reconstructed the church that stood on this site and dedicated it to St James. It has been largely remodelled over the centuries, and only became a cathedral in 1914.

In one sense, I have come full circle in walking from Thetford Priory to St Edmund's Abbey. The first was the burial site

Above: St Edmundsbury Cathedral and (**top**) the ruins of the original abbey church.

ot Henry VIII's son, the second was that of his favourite sister, Mary Tudor. She is buried in St Mary's church (dedicated to the Virgin rather than to her) which is part of the abbey complex. Her tomb was moved from the abbey church at the Dissolution. So Henry's destruction of the monasteries had very personal repercussions: it shifted the remains of both his sister and son.

I return to the circular park behind the Great Gateway, take a seat and pull out my sandwiches. As I do, bouncing in from stage left comes a muntjac. No one takes any notice, so I assume this happens all the time. It skitters over the flower beds and exits stage right. I wonder... the muntjacs

Above: Post-Reformation, houses were crafted from the ruins of the monastery.

that seem to have been shadowing me... could they in fact be just the one creature? A pilgrim Bambi that has bounced along beside me all the way?

THE MYSTERIOUS ST EDMUND

Edmund was a king who became a saint, yet is something of a mystery figure. Indeed, one of the greatest mysteries surrounding him is what happened to his body, which had disappeared from his shrine by the time the priory was suppressed in 1539.

This king of East Anglia was martyred in 870 by pagan Danish invaders for refusing to renounce his faith, for which he was tied to a tree, turned into a pincushion by archers, and then decapitated. Where his martyrdom occurred is not known, but in 903 his body was brought to Bury. A thousand years ago, in 1020, King Canute build a shrine for him in the town. When, in 1095, the great abbey church was built, St Edmund's relics were moved to a bejewelled, gold and silver embellished shrine within it. For centuries it was visited by pilgrims, from kings to commoners.

By the cathedral is a bronze statue of St Edmund by Elisabeth Frink, unveiled in 1976.

It is known his body was in the shrine in 1198, when it was opened after being damaged by fire. At some point between then and 1539 it was removed, perhaps by the prior and monks when they realised the abbey was bound to fall to Henry VIII's desecrators. There is a theory that Edmund's remains were placed in an iron chest and reburied somewhere in the abbey's 14-acre gardens.

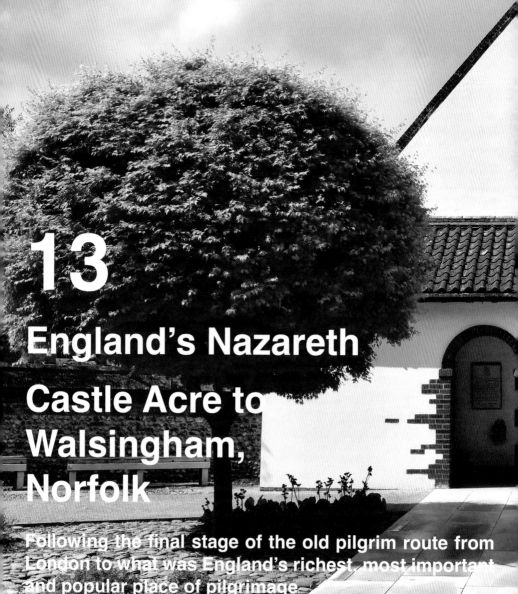

13

England's Nazareth

Castle Acre to Walsingham, Norfolk

Following the final stage of the old pilgrim route from London to what was England's richest, most important and popular place of pilgrimage

The Anglican Shrine, Walsingham

A fantastical tale brought pilgrims, from kings and queens to commoners, to Walsingham in the Middle Ages. In 1061 a Walsingham noblewoman, Lady Richeldis, had a vision in which the Virgin Mary transported her soul to Nazareth and showed her the house where the Holy Family once lived, and in which the Annunciation of Archangel Gabriel, foretelling Jesus's birth, occurred.

Lady Richeldis was told to build a replica of the house in Walsingham. The resulting Holy House, incredibly richly decorated with gold and precious jewels, became a shrine and attracted pilgrims to Walsingham from all over Europe.

The shrine was completely destroyed at the time of the Dissolution, but its site is marked in the grounds of the ruined Walsingham Abbey. Today, some 300,000 come each year to Walsingham, and there are Anglican, Catholic and Orthodox shrines in the village. The Catholic shrine is in the Slipper Chapel, a mile from the Holy House, where pilgrims would leave their shoes and continue barefoot.

In the Middle Ages, Castle Acre was the final night's stop before Walsingham on the pilgrim route from London. The place would have been bustling, packed with pilgrims eagerly anticipating their arrival at what was by far England's richest, most important and popular place of pilgrimage. Today, Walsingham is once again our premier shrine, but Castle Acre – a Norman fortified town established by a knight who had fought alongside William the Conqueror at Hastings – is largely overlooked, a shadow of the important medieval pilgrim town it once was.

I like all that about Castle Acre. I don't want my pilgrimage to make me part of a group, even a devout and pious one. And I also like the fact that there is no official route; no Pilgrim's Way, all waymarked and clear-cut. So the route I'll take you along for the next two days is one I have created, from the evidence available, and designed to link the most interesting places along the way, including a fine example of a Norfolk round tower church, an abandoned medieval village, plus a sleepy market town and tracts of the finest countryside.

As Castle Acre is over 21 miles from Walsingham, it seems likely that pilgrims on their last night of travel would have been riding rather than walking. So I propose an overnight stay a few miles short of Walsingham, giving plenty of time on the second day to explore its many riches.

PRACTICAL INFORMATION

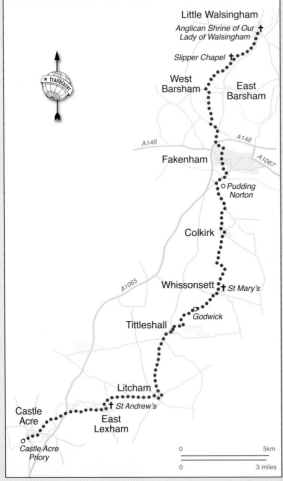

- **Terrain** Mainly quiet lanes and some footpaths over gently undulating countryside.
- **Difficulty** Moderate
- **Directions & GPS***
013.pdf, 013.gpx, 013.kml at
🖥 https://trailblazer-guides
.com/press
  * See p10-11 for more information on downloads

ROUTE OVERVIEW
21.4 miles (34.4km)

This is a walk across a truly historic landscape with big skies, following in the footsteps of many thousands of pilgrims over hundreds of years. There is much to see and contemplate in Walsingham so allow plenty of time there.

Castle Acre to Fakenham
15.5 miles (24.9km)

- **Time** 6 hrs actual walking time
- **Total ascent** 210m/690ft
- **Map** OS Explorer *238 Dereham & Aylsham*

From Castle Acre for the **3.7 miles** to East Lexham the route follows the Nar Valley Way, a long-distance route from King's Lynn to Gressenhall. Its green on white roundels depicting a river and trees are a useful guide to this part of the route. You then take to quiet lanes over gently undulating countryside, reaching Litcham in **1.9 miles**, Tittleshall in **2.7 miles**, the abandoned village of Godwick in **1.1 miles**, Whissonsett in **1.6 miles**, Colkirk in **2.1** miles, and Fakenham in **2.4** miles.

Fakenham to Walsingham   5.9 miles (9.5km)

● **Time** 1hr 30 mins actual walking time ● **Total ascent** 53m/175ft
● **Map** OS Explorer *251 Norfolk Coast Central*

Today's walk is short, to ensure you have plenty of time to explore all that Walsingham has to offer. It is just **4 miles** along quiet lanes from Fakenham to the Slipper Chapel, the Catholic shrine, after which a footpath follows an old railway track for the final Holy Mile – actually **1.9 miles** on this route, but preferable to the often-busy lane into Walsingham.

Day walk options

For the energetic, complete the entire route in one day. Or, for a gentle walk that will leave plenty of time to enjoy Walsingham, start from Fakenham.
● **By public transport** Take the train to King's Lynn station then a bus or taxi to Castle Acre to begin the walk. If starting from Fakenham take a bus or taxi from King's Lynn station. From Walsingham take a taxi back to King's Lynn station.
● **Taxi option** Near and Far (☎ 01328-853636, ▣ nearandfarfakenham.co.uk)

Where to eat or stay along the way

● **Castle Acre** Stay overnight at former pub *Old Red Lion* ☎ 01760-755557, ▣ oldredlion.org.uk, Bailey St), now a hostel, or the *Ostrich Inn* (☎ 01760-755398, ▣ ostrich-castleacre.com, Stocks Green), a 16th century coaching inn.
● **Litcham** Have **lunch** at the *Bull Hotel* (☎ 01328-701340, ▣ thelitchambull.co.uk, 1 Church St) or grab the ingredients for a picnic at *Litcham Post Office Stores* (Church St; Mon-Sat 7.30am-7pm, Sun 9am-1pm) from its in-store bakery.
● **Fakenham** Stay by the river at the *Wensum Lodge Hotel* (☎ 01328-862100, ▣ wensumlodge.co.uk, Bridge St), part of a former mill dating from 1750.
● **Walsingham** Celebrate your pilgrimage at the **Anglican Shrine's** *Norton Café Bar* (▣ walsinghamanglican.org.uk/visit/nortons-cafe-bar) which offers everything from a cooked breakfast to lunch, evening meal, coffee and cakes.

PILGRIMAGE HIGHLIGHTS

● Visit the round tower church of **St Andrew, East Lexham** (daily dawn to dusk)
● Feel the history of the abandoned medieval village at **Godwick**.
● In **Walsingham** visit the **Catholic shrine**, (▣ walsingham.org.uk, Houghton St Giles; the ruins of **Walsingham Priory** (▣ walsinghamabbey.com, Common Pl; daily 11am-4pm); and the spot where the Holy House stood; the **Anglican Shrine** (▣ walsinghamanglican.org.uk, 2 Common Pl); and the **Orthodox Shrine** (Station Rd; Sat,Wed 2pm-4pm).

*Saints' feast days There are numerous pilgrimage dates to Walsingham, key among them are: **Anglican pilgrimage**: late May Bank Holiday*
***Feast of Our Lady of Walsingham**: Catholic: 24 September; Anglican: 15 October*

13

Castle Acre

Castle Acre is a village in a town's trousers. It's just a shadow of the rotund, massively important medieval pilgrim town it once was. Now it's just a skinny little village, and its trousers – ok, the great stone defensive walls that encompass it – stand right out, with plenty of air between belt and belly.

I pass through the Bailey Gate to find a quiet village street, a church, and a great deal of green open space. At one end of the area enclosed by the remnants of those robust walls are the substantial ruins of Castle Acre Priory, once in the hands of the Cluniac order, renowned as pilgrim hosts. At the other, the remnants of the castle. There would have been dozens of pilgrim hostelries, now there's just the Ostrich, and the Old Red Lion.

Castle Acre to East Lexham

I hitch a ride out of Castle Acre on a long-distance path called the Nar Valley Way, which runs through Norfolk from King's Lynn to Gressenhall, here sunken between hedgerows that close overhead to form a green tunnel. It's a place for pilgrim reverie, in which I am happily indulging when a branch reaches out and pings my glasses off. So I'm down on my knees, a little earlier than expected, scrabbling among the leaves for those specs, muttering not so much prayers but, I'm sorry to admit, ripe curses. You can always trust Mother Nature to take a cocky pilgrim down a peg or two.

Glasses retrieved, I look up to see a flock of black, curly-horned sheep watching me indifferently behind a gate which warns 'Beware of the bull'. There is further photogenic animal life at

The ruins of Castle Acre Priory

Newton Mill, where a swan has built its nest on an islet in the middle of the River Nar, with the old brick bridge and a row of flint cottages making the perfect backdrop.

Then comes another green way, wider this time, and the first of many quiet lanes I shall follow. The sun gets his hat on, allowing the oak and copper beech that line the way to shuffle dappled shadow patterns at my feet. The lane has grass growing down the centre, which classifies it as a walkers' road in my book. It takes me to the village of East Lexham, where the sun-

shine abruptly falters. Hail pelts down, bringing the white blossom from the trees down with it. As abruptly as the storm arrived, it departs.

East Lexham and the round-tower church of St Andrew

Crossing East Lexham's village green, with its jaunty witch's-hat of a shelter, I round a corner to reach a farmyard, just beyond which is something rarely seen outside East Anglia: a round-tower church. At 900 years

Above: St Andrew's Church, East Lexham

old, St Andrew's is Saxon, and a perfect place for a Walsingham pilgrim to stop by.

From the lane, at first glimpse, it looks like the turret of a Norman castle but approaching you see that a nave is tacked on to it. The render makes the main church look a good deal younger than the rough flint tower, although it probably isn't. As I admire it, the church clock chimes delicately, like the triangle in a percussion section. Inside it is wonderfully simple, with its pitch pine pews and whitewashed walls.

I love these churches, and the mystery of why they have round towers. To my knowledge there is no definitive explanation. What is certain is that this is one of the oldest churches in England, and its position on a mound within a circular churchyard suggests that it may have been

THE ROYAL PATH TO WALSINGHAM

A string of kings travelled as pilgrims from Castle Acre to Walsingham: Henry III, who made a dozen visits from 1226; his son Edward I, who matched his tally; and Edward III, a regular supporter of the shrine between 1328 and 1361.

From 1509, Henry VIII gave generous gifts of gold, and made regular payments for a priest to sing before Our Lady of Walsingham. He came several times, once walking barefoot the final mile from the Slipper Chapel. Catherine of Aragon was a regular pilgrim, and Anne Boleyn planned to come, but accounts differ as to whether she made it.

Such royal patronage drove Walsingham's popular appeal. In the 15th and early 16th centuries it eclipsed even St Thomas Becket's popularity at Canterbury. When, in the 1530s, Walsingham's annual income was assessed prior to its suppression, £250 came from offerings made 'in the chapel of the Blessed Virgin Mary', which contrasted with just over £32 received at the shrine of St Thomas.

plonked on top of a pagan site. From here I depart from the Nar Valley Way, and take the lanes through the woods, and then the B road to Litcham, and lunch.

Litcham

Litcham is a village on a crossroads, and a key staging post for medieval Walsingham pilgrims. Five ancient routes, including the still very current B1145 King's Lynn to Norwich road, converge here.

Priory Farmhouse is on the site of a medieval hermitage and contains the remnants of a 14th century priory. All Saints' church has a puzzling piece of medieval graffiti, known as the Litcham Cryptogram, carved into a pillar. Believed to have been cut by a Walsingham pilgrim, it is hard to decipher and open to various interpretations, but one is that the top line of lettering, 'a s .j. m a y', stands for 'anima salv. jesu. maria a yosephu' which translates as 'save (my) soul Jesus, Mary and Joseph'. The first two letters of the lower line, 'm m', may refer to 'memento mori': you must die, but the meaning of the rest

of the line, 'wyke baumburgh' is pretty much anyone's guess.

Litcham offers all the hungry and thirsty contemporary pilgrim might need: the Bull Inn, a general store and post office, plus butcher.

It's all sky between Litcham and Tittleshall. Spread above me like a cloud atlas, I count cumulus, stratus, cirrostratus and altocumulus before I get confused and decide it is time to stride on.

Godwick to Fakenham

There is a ghostly crossroads in the medieval village of Godwick. The church tower, the Great Barn and the remains of Godwick Hall are the main reminders of a village abandoned in the 1600s because, depending on who you believe, either the land was too poor to support reliable harvests or the peasants were ousted in favour of more remunerative sheep. Standing on the grass before the ruined tower of All Saints' church, I learn that this was once the main street. To either side of the church other lanes ran off, one to Greenstein, the other to Sutton, both also now deserted.

From here, the path follows what was once a lane leading to the next village, Whissonsett. In the church, St Mary's, a niche in the wall of the nave contains the head of a very rare 10th century Anglo Saxon Cross, which was uncovered by grave diggers in the church yard in 1902. It is the only example of an interlaced wheel design in Norfolk and may date from around 920.

Above: Marker at the abandoned village of Godwick. **Below**: The path north of Godwick.

I wind through Colkirk then along the lanes to skirt Pudding Norton, another abandoned medieval village, where the ruined tower of St Margaret's church protrudes like a broken tooth above the hedgerows. On the outskirts of Fakenham, the remains of St Stephen's Priory, founded as a hospital in the 12th century, are little more than bumps in the grass. Once pilgrims would have found shelter here. Today, I suggest continuing over the River Wensum and picking one of the pubs or B&Bs in the sleepy market town of Fakenham.

Fakenham to North Barsham

I want a full day to experience Walsingham, so am up early for the climb out of town, then over the A148 for a brief stint on the B1105 before escaping onto the quiet lanes medieval pilgrims would have taken. Alternatively, you could stick to the B road and travel via East Barsham, but there is no pavement and the road can be busy.

Much better to wind your way through the hamlet of West Barsham, with its little 12th century flint church of the Assumption of the Blessed Virgin Mary, and then alongside the water meadows through which the River Stiffkey trickles to North

Barsham with its 13th century church of All Saints. Depopulation from the 16th century meant these villages, and their churches, shrank from the significant pilgrimage staging posts they once were. Now begins the final, sacred approach to Walsingham.

Slipper Chapel, Houghton St Giles

The Slipper Chapel, which houses the Catholic Shrine of Our Lady of Walsingham, announces itself with the appearance through the trees of a great barn of a modern church, but just beyond it is a small wayside chapel that is the only surviving remnant of the ancient shrine of Walsingham, dating from 1360. The Slipper Chapel marks the boundary of Walsingham's sacred space and is where medieval pilgrims removed their shoes to walk the last 'Holy Mile' to Walsingham barefoot.

From the meadows it looks like a stumpy little flint rocket ready for blast off. It's tiny and only a few pilgrims at a time can shuffle into its cool interior. You wouldn't know it today, but it suffered a long period of secular use. Thomas Cromwell, who did such a thorough job of obliterating the Holy House just

Below: The Slipper Chapel

down the lane at Walsingham Abbey, left it alone, and it survived to be used as a poor house, a forge, a cowshed and a barn. An 1894 photograph shows cows grazing peacefully outside.

Then it was rescued. In 1895, wealthy local woman Charlotte Pearson Boyd bought the building, had it converted back to ecclesiastical use and gave it to the Catholic Church. In 1934 the Slipper Chapel was designated the 'National Shrine of Our Lady for Roman Catholics in England'. After a gap of 300 years, Walsingham was once again a place of pilgrimage.

Walsingham

I don't take my boots off for the final Holy Mile, on a footpath that follows the track of an old railway, but do feel the power of the place I am entering. Walsingham really does feel like a holy village, as well as being lovely, with its honeyed stone. Halfway down the High Street stands the still-majestic gateway to the 11th century priory of Our Lady of Walsingham. A grill in the door offers a perspective through the trees to the soaring arch that once framed the east window of the abbey church. Pop round

the corner to enter via the Georgian Shire-hall, a pilgrim hostel in the 15th century, and you pass through a belt of trees to enter a glade in which the ruined abbey stands.

Before that east window a modest little board marks the place where the shrine of the Holy House of Nazareth once stood. Not a scrap of it remains, an indication of the fear its power instilled in Henry VIII and Cromwell.

Around the corner in Holt Road is the Anglican Shrine of Our Lady of Walsingham. It was built in the 1930s, so has no intrinsic history of its own, but enter and you find a remarkable modern replica of the original Holy House. During building work, a minor miracle occurred: they discovered a well, producing a steady flow of pure, clear water, and it was incorporated into the church.

Church of the Annunciation, Walsingham

In 2008, the Orthodox church established the charming little pilgrim chapel of St Seraphim in Walsingham's former railway station, with an icon of Christ above the door and the roof topped with a dome and cross.

All of this makes Walsingham one of the most satisfying pilgrim destinations, and a little time devoted to exploring it will be richly rewarded.

THE HOLY HOUSE

The Holy House was built in either the 11th or 12th centuries, (accounts differ), and was made of wood. In the 1500s, however, a stone chapel was carefully wrapped around the original. An account by Erasmus, the Renaissance scholar and Christian philosopher, gives us a very clear picture of what pilgrims found here. Within the stone chapel, he writes, 'there is a small chapel built on a wooden platform. Pilgrims are admitted through a narrow door on each side. There is very little light: only what comes from tapers, which have a most pleasing scent... and if you peer inside... you would say it was the abode of saints, so dazzling is it with jewels, gold, and silver'.

Of the statue of Virgin and Child, he writes: 'there was a dim religious light, and she stood in the shadows to the right of the altar... a small image... unimpressive in size, material and workmanship but of surpassing power.'

Erasmus says that pilgrims visited other points in the abbey, including holy wells to the east of the priory church. On the altar of the priory church was a crystal phial said to contain Mary's sacred milk.

A contemporary ballad, *The Walsingham Lament* expressed the sense of loss at the Dissolution: 'Weepe, weepe O Walsingham, whose days are nightes,
Blessings turn to blasphemies, holy deeds to dispites.'

14

St Milburga's Shropshire

Ironbridge, Much Wenlock, Wenlock Edge

A circular route along the River Severn from Ironbridge, taking in two ruined abbeys and climbing the dramatic limestone escarpment of Wenlock Edge

Ironbridge must have been a grimy, cacophonous place once but, today, as I head out of town along the Severn Way, the only man-made din is the clanking from the demolition team dismantling the old power station across the river. The area's industrial past seems as remote as the days of medieval pilgrimage to the shrine and holy well of St Milburga.

In the Middle Ages, many thousands of pilgrims travelled over the Shropshire Hills to Much Wenlock, to the priory where Milburga had been abbess, and where her holy well was imbued with the power to cure eye diseases. On this walk I make a rather round-about pilgrimage to it, in order to enjoy the wonderful countryside to the full.

Pastoral scene after Wenlock Priory

PRACTICAL INFORMATION

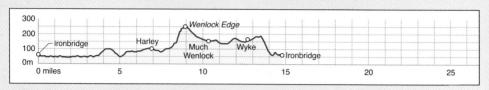

- **Terrain** Gently rolling countryside, apart from the steep and sustained climb up Wenlock Edge
- **Difficulty** Easy, with a moderate stretch climbing Wenlock Edge
- **Directions & GPS*** 014.pdf, 014.gpx, 014.kml at ⊟ https://trailblazer-guides.com/press

* See p10-11 for more information on downloads

ROUTE OVERVIEW   14.8 miles (23.8km)

Taking in sections of three different long-distance paths, this walk combines stunning scenery and historical pilgrimage with the area's important industrial heritage. A short second stage allows plenty of time to explore Much Wenlock and Ironbridge at either end.

Ironbridge to Much Wenlock via Harley   10.4 miles (16.7km)

- **Time** 3hrs 45mins actual walking time
- **Total ascent** 360m / 181ft
- **Map** OS Explorer *242 Telford, Ironbridge & The Wrekin; 241 Shrewsbury; 217 The Long Mynd & Wenlock Edge*

Beginning in Ironbridge, at the south side of the Iron Bridge itself, walk across and pick up the Severn Way temporarily as it runs alongside the River Severn for **2.2 miles** to Buildwas, after which it is a gentle walk across farmland and through woods via Sheinton (**2.5 miles**) to Harley, reached after **2.2 miles**. The route follows quiet lanes between fields until, after **1.5 miles**, you begin the steep, sustained ascent on a woodland droving road to the summit of Wenlock Edge, reached after a further **0.6 mile**. From here it is a gentle descent to the town of Much Wenlock, in **1.4 miles**.

Much Wenlock to Ironbridge via Wyke   4.4 miles (7.1km)

- **Time** 1hr 30mins actual walking time
- **Total ascent** 142m / 466ft
- **Map** OS Explorer *242 Telford, Ironbridge & The Wrekin*

This shorter, relaxed walk begins with an amble over farmland via Wyke (**2.4 miles**) along the Shropshire Way, its signs featuring a bird of prey, to reach the opposite bank of the Severn to that taken on the first section of the walk, arriving back at the Iron Bridge in **2 miles**.

Day walk options

This circular walk could be completed in a day, starting and ending at Ironbridge.

● **By public transport** Take the train to Telford station, then a bus or taxi to the start at Ironbridge.

● **Taxi option** Diamond Cars, Telford (☎ 01952-222222, 💻 diamond cars.co.uk)

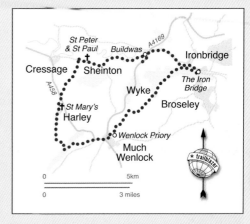

Where to eat or stay

● **Ironbridge** Stay at the *Bridge View Guest House* (☎ 01952-432541, 💻 iron-bridgeview.co.uk, 10 Tontine Hill) right on the Gorge and **eat** fine Indian food at *Pondicherry* (☎ 01952-433055, 💻 pondicherry restaurant.co.uk; 57 Waterloo St).

● **Much Wenlock** Stay overnight at *The Fox Inn* (☎ 01952-727292, 💻 foxinnmuch wenlock.co.uk, 46 High St), a warm and welcoming pub with good grub. Have afternoon tea at *Tea on the Square* (☎ 01952-727929, 💻 facebook.com/Tea-on-the-Square, 21 Barrow St).

PILGRIMAGE HIGHLIGHTS

● Walk to the tranquil riverside remains of **Buildwas Abbey** (💻 english-heritage.org.uk/visit/places/buildwas-abbey/; Apr-Oct 10am-5pm, Nov-Mar Tue-Sat 10am-4pm).

● Climb the ancient pilgrim path over **Wenlock Edge** and be rewarded with stunning views from the top.

● Explore the lovely medieval town of Much Wenlock, and visit **Wenlock Priory** (💻 english-heritage.org.uk/visit/places/wenlock-priory/; Apr-Sept 10am-6pm, Oct-3 Nov 10am-5pm, 4 Nov-16 Feb 10am-4pm, 5 Sheinton Street).

St Milburga's saint's day: 23 February

14

Above: The Iron Bridge.

Ironbridge

In the early morning sunlight, the bridge that spans the River Severn, and which gives Ironbridge its name, seems a rather frail looking thing, considering the transformation it caused. To find the catalyst for the Industrial Revolution in this peaceful, wooded gorge seems misplaced.

There are scullers on the mirror-still river far beneath the bridge's red tracery span, and the polite chimes of St Luke's sound more suited to a parlour mantlepiece clock. Surely, the world's first cast iron bridge (built in 1779) should have been slung over some fetid canal in a grimy industrial heartland?

The Severn Way runs alongside the slow brown river upstream of Ironbridge, but has to link back to the road when bits of the industrial past hinder its passage. It is narrow and perilously close to the river in a couple of places and, if it is wet underfoot, is best forsaken for the pavement. No matter, you are soon crossing the river and arriving at Buildwas Abbey.

Buildwas Abbey

The ruins of Buildwas, a 12th century Cistercian house, hunker down beside the Severn. The Cistercians built plain abbeys in remote spots, and the monks lived austere lives in which manual labour was almost as important as the life of the spirit. Today, this still feels like a cloistered spot. The abbey church, open to the heavens and with a lush green carpet, has great muscular pillars lining the nave, as stout as those at Durham Cathedral. I wander

Right and below: Buildwas Abbey

around the cloister and duck into the beautiful, vaulted chapter house with its remarkably well-preserved tiled floor.

A little way up the main road is the turning to Mill Farm where, despite a sign insisting this is a 'Footpath Only', you pick up a quiet, traffic-free lane that lopes from farm to farm along the valley, between the river and AE Housman's 'blue remembered hills'. Then comes Sheinton, where the church of St Peter and St Paul stands high on a natural mound, shepherding its little flock of cottages. I turn onto a bridleway where the cow parsley on the verge serves as a lacy border to the great, yellow-block fields of oil seed rape and it takes me, arrow-straight, to Harley.

Harley

Harley is a Thankful Village, one of only 53 parishes in England and Wales to suffer no casualties in World War I. So, instead of a roll of honour for the dead, there is a plaque in

14

13th century St Mary's church listing those who returned safely, and an inscribed bench in the churchyard, where I take a rest and enjoy the distant prospect of Wenlock Edge, which I shall be yomping up later.

I notice the grave of Kenneth John Allden, on which the inscription reads: 'On a perfect day when the sky is pure blue, gaze at The Edge in the distance and think of me'. As it happens, the day is perfect, the sky is blue, so I do.

At Christmas a Festival of Light is held at St Mary's, with around 15 Christmas trees in the church, candles everywhere, and a star-like beacon on top of the church tower which can be picked out from the summit of Wenlock Edge.

Wenlock Edge

In the fields towards Domas the growing wheat is rising in a green tide, and the broad beans emerging as a network of florets on the sandy soil. The lane dips down, and wooded Wenlock Edge rears up before me. The deep-sunk track up this narrow limestone escarpment takes an oblique approach, but still runs at a gradient to raise the heart-rate of the drovers and pack-horse men who came this way for so many centuries, and challenge the commitment of the pilgrims who shared their route in the Middle Ages. Once crested, the edge takes a gentle path over bare limestone towards Much Wenlock,

Below: Sheinton Church. **Right**: St Milburga's Well now lies neglected in Much Wenlock.

SISTERS IN SAINTHOOD

St Milburga's story is a familiar one among female saints, and echoes those of St Mildred from Walk 1, St Frideswide from Walk 9, and St Winefride from Walk 17. Like her sisters in sainthood, Milburga was a noblewoman who fled the attentions of a prince determined to marry her against her will, escaping across a river which then suddenly, miraculously, became so swollen that his pursuit was foiled.

Clearly this cannot be the literal truth for each of these saints. Rather, it is a recurrent myth, in which women resist sexual violence and go on to become powerful, independent figures. All three became abbesses, and as such had great power and independence, meeting nobles on equal terms. They were not the chattels of their husbands, as other women were. Incidentally, speaking of sisters in sainthood, St Mildred was St Milburga's actual, biological older sister. It's a small world, Anglo Saxon sainthood.

which is laid out in the valley before me.

Wenlock Edge, a unique limestone escarpment over 19 miles long and a site of special scientific interest because of its geology, was among the inspirations for AE Housman's collection of poems, *A Shropshire Lad*, and six were set to music in Ralph Vaughan Williams' *On Wenlock Edge*. If you like music while you walk, they make a perfect soundtrack to this stretch of the route.

Much Wenlock

The lovely medieval town of Much Wenlock owes its existence to its priory, and St Milburga. On this bright day it is bustling with visitors, but from the 12th to the 16th centuries it was pilgrims who thronged the town.

Milburga had a gift for healing, particularly for restoring sight to the blind. Miraculous cures were attributed to her holy well, but it is an almost forgotten pilgrim point today. I hunt it down, eventually finding it tucked out of sight in a side passageway off Barrow St. I had hoped to discover a tumbling spring of clear water, but find a dry, brick-lined, weed-choked pit. There is a gate in the low wrought iron fence that protects it, and steps down to a low archway. Above the arch is an inscription obscured by ivy. I peel the tendrils back and can just make out the words 'St Milburga's Well'. To me, there is a

poignancy in discovering a once-venerated place that is now overlooked. It reminds me that to be a pilgrim in 21st century England is often to forge a way along a path trodden by few in recent years.

Why is it dry? This well-head dates from 1897, and it's not certain it was the actual holy well, but the Victorians who restored it were trusting to local legend. In 1913 this and other wells were drained into the sewers as part of a scheme to end flooding in the town, which sits at the bottom of a bowl.

Waking back up Barrow St to Wilmore St, I pass the parish church of Holy Trinity, built on the site of St Milburga's nuns' church (her monks had another). Here the saint was buried, beside the altar but, over the centuries, forgotten. Then, the story goes, in 1101 two boys fell through the church floor and her bones and the remains of her coffin were rediscovered. The relics were transferred to the priory, and the pilgrims flocked.

The priory is just down the Bull Ring, on the path I will take to continue my walk. Just before it is a square tower, all that remains of the original monastery boundary wall, and one of two that stood either side of the entrance gates.

Wenlock Priory

Even in its ruined state, the priory is impressive. The church was the size of a cathedral, and large sections of its 13th century walls still stand to roof height, rising from manicured lawns, amid topiary-lined avenues. St Milburga's bones were transferred to a shrine at the east end of the church, behind the high altar.

One unusual feature of the priory was the communal lavatorium, an octagonal building supporting a central cistern from which water flowed through a series of carved heads into a shallow trough, allow-

The ruins of Wenlock Priory

ing 16 monks to wash simultaneously before meals.

The lavatorium would have been decorated with carved panels, and two remain – or, rather, reproductions of them remain here, the originals are in Much Wenlock's museum at the corner of High St and Wilmore St. The stones depict Christ and the Apostles. One shows Christ calling Peter and Andrew on the Sea of Galilee with James and John in another boat, the other portrays John and another apostle whose identity is uncertain.

From Much Wenlock the walk is a gentle glide through meadows, following the

Shropshire Way, with just the hamlet of Wyke and the farm at The Vineyards before the easy descent to the wooded Ironbridge Gorge, the river Severn and the final stretch along a disused railway to the bridge from which I set out.

THE STORY OF WENLOCK PRIORY

Wenlock Priory was founded in 680 by the Anglo-Saxon noble Merewald, who installed his daughter Milburga as abbess. She was in charge of a community of both monks and nuns and her status as the local ruler was later confirmed by King Ethelred of Mercia. The priory also owned all the land in the area, so Milburga's reputation as a miraculous protector of harvests would have been of significance to the many peasant farmers who were under her jurisdiction. In this, her myth may elide with that of a local pagan goddess, a grain protectress who could no longer be venerated once the area had been Christianised.

The priory also had a social mission. Ashfield Hall in Much Wenlock High St is on the site of the 13th century St John's Hospital, the medieval monastic hospital for 'lost and naked beggars' and the street's then name, Spittle St, derived from the hospital.

After the Norman Conquest the priory was put under the control of the French Benedictine monastery of Cluny, and dedicated to St Michael and St Milburga. Once St Milburga's relics were discovered, Much Wenlock became a major regional pilgrimage centre. It was closed down in 1540 during Henry VIII's Dissolution of the Monasteries.

15

St Paulinus
and the Ebor Way

Wetherby to York

Following two rivers and the course of a Roman road, over gentle Yorkshire countryside, in the footsteps of York's first bishop

Two rivers and the course of a Roman road take me from Wetherby to York, and there can be no finer or more appropriate way to approach that city. The route I follow is called the Ebor Way, from *Eboracum*, the Roman name for York, and was travelled by St Paulinus, the city's Roman first bishop, as he Christianised the North.

This walk follows one of the finest stretches of the Ebor Way, which was developed in the 1970s by the Ebor Acorn Rambling Club, and takes you through great, easy-walking country. There is a pleasant rhythm to the walk between the riverside towns of Wetherby and Tadcaster; a sustained contemplative stretch along the isolated, solitary Roman road from Tadcaster to the outskirts of York; and a further peaceful riverside stretch on the approach to that city.

Once in York, the path takes you via two unusual pilgrim places – a secret church and the home and the shrine to St Margaret Clitherow, the 'Pearl of York' – and the scene of the terrible massacre of York's Jewish population who, in 1190, were trapped by a mob in the castle known as Clifford's Tower. Then comes the grand finale of York Minster, the largest Gothic cathedral in northern Europe.

The River Wharfe near Tadcaster Bridge

PRACTICAL INFORMATION

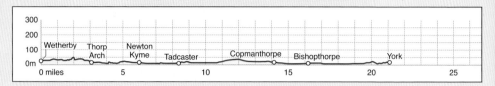

- **Terrain** Mainly earth footpaths, with some city and town pavements
- **Difficulty** Easy
- **Directions & GPS*** 015.pdf, 015.gpx, 015.kml at 🖳 https://trailblazer-guides.com/press

        * See p10-11 for more information on downloads

ROUTE OVERVIEW   21.1 miles (33.9km)

Gentle riverside walking at its finest, taking in a stretch of the Ebor Way and an ancient Roman road, culminating in a stunning aerial view of the city from the top of York Minster tower. Allow plenty of time for the sights of York.

Wetherby to Tadcaster   8.3 miles (13.3km)
- **Time** 2½ hours actual walking time
- **Total Ascent** 90m/295ft
- **Map** OS Explorer 289 Leeds

The route to York, over gentle, almost flat Yorkshire farmland, follows the Ebor Way, although its white-on-green roundels depicting York Minster are missing at some key points. From Wetherby the route is over farmland until, after **3 miles**, at Thorp Arch, the path follows the banks of the River Wharfe for **5.3 miles** to Tadcaster.

Tadcaster to York   12.8 miles (20.6km)
- **Time** 4½ hours actual walking time   - **Total Ascent** 163m/535ft
- **Map** OS Explorer 290 York

From Tadcaster you take the die-straight route of The Old Street, a Roman road, for **6.2 miles** to Copmanthorpe, then over the fields for **2.2 miles** to Bishopthorpe, where you join a second river, the Ouse, for a **4.4 mile** walk along its banks to the city.

Day walk options
- **By public transport** For the Wetherby to Tadcaster section, take the train to Leeds and a bus or taxi from Leeds station to begin the walk at Wetherby. At Tadcaster take a bus or taxi back to Leeds. For the Tadcaster to York stretch, take the train to York, then a bus or taxi to begin at Tadcaster.
- **Taxi option** York Station Taxis (☎ 01904-623332, 🖳 yorkstationtaxis.co.uk).

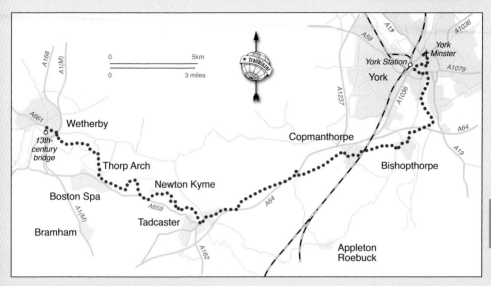

Where to stay or eat along the way

● **Wetherby** **Stay** before the walk at elegant *Wharfe House B&B* in the town centre (☎ 01937-588819, 🖳 wharfe.house, Westgate).
● **Tadcaster** **Stay** at the *Shann House Hotel* (☎ 01937-833931; 🖳 samuelsmithshotels .co.uk/shann-house-hotel-tadcaster) a Georgian townhouse B&B run by the Tadcaster's Sam Smith brewery. **Drink** at the *Angel and White Horse* (☎ 01937-835470).
● **York** Numerous places to stay and eat in the city centre.

PILGRIMAGE HIGHLIGHTS

● Admire the 13th century engineering of the stone **bridge** over the River Wharfe at **Wetherby**.
● In **York**, acknowledge the darker side of faith by visiting three sites associated with religious oppression: The hidden Catholic chapel at the **Bar Convent** (🖳 bar-convent.org.uk; Mon-Sat 10am-4pm, Sun closed, 17 Blossom Street), the scene of an anti-Semitic atrocity at **Clifford's Tower** (🖳 english-heritage.org.uk/ visit/places/cliffords-tower-york, Tower St YO1 9SA) and the **shrine of St Margaret Clitherow**, (🖳 stwilfridsyork.org.uk/shrine-st-margaret-clitherow; Mon-Sat 9.30am-5pm, Sun 8am-5pm, 35 The Shambles).
Enjoy the awe-inspiring view from the top of **York Minister** (🖳 yorkminster.org; Mon-Thur 11am-4:30pm; Fri & Sat 10am-4:30pm; Sun 12.30–2.30pm; Deangate).

Saints' days: St Paulinus 10 October; St William of York 8 June

Wetherby

The weir upstream of the venerable, 13th century bridge at Wetherby makes the Wharfe a very busy river. The waters are swirling through the four wide stone arches that once took the Great North Road through this coaching town, then fanning out and threatening to overtop the wellies of the children who are paddling in the shallows. They squeal in fearful delight.

The river will be with me for most of the stretch to Tadcaster, but for now I must leave it as I strike north then east and out of town, passing above six blaring lanes of

ST PAULINUS

Paulinus was a young Roman monk who accompanied St Augustine on his mission to bring Christianity to the Anglo Saxons (see Walk 1). In around 625 he travelled north from Kent with Ethelburga, sister of the king of Kent, when she married Edwin, king of Northumbria. Ethelburga was Christian, Edwin was not, but Paulinus succeeded in converting the king. He also baptised a future saint, Hilda of Whitby (see Walk 18).

Pope Gregory, who had sent Augustine and Paulinus to England, had decreed that the second metropolitan *see* (the main area of ecclesiastical jurisdiction), after Canterbury, should be established in York. Paulinus built a church here, but no trace of it survives. He also travelled extensively in this region and built many other churches.

When Edwin was killed in a battle against the Welsh and Mercians (from the Midlands) in 633 his kingdom was split. Christianity suffered a severe decline, and Paulinus fled south, becoming Bishop of Rochester. Gregory had determined to make Paulinus Archbishop of York, but the *pallium* (the woollen vestment confirming that status) did not arrive until after he had left the North.

It was not until Edwin's successor, Oswald, brought Aidan to his kingdom that Christianity gained a lasting footing in the region (see Walk 19). After Paulinus's death, in 644, he was canonised, and is now venerated in the Anglican, Roman Catholic and Eastern Orthodox churches.

the A1 and onto the blessed peace of a green road, Heuthwaite Lane. I meet the Wharfe again, briefly, at Flint Mill Grange, but we don't get together properly until the hamlet of Thorp Arch, after which we become firm friends almost all the way to Tadcaster.

I can't help noticing that the river has changed character since we were last together. It is calmer, more mature, and positively stately as it glides past the outskirts of Boston Spa. On its banks at Town Ings

are two remnants of the spa that gave Boston the other half of its name.

The first is a row of very neat stone bungalows right on the bank, which were once a bath house, tea room and pump house. On the other side of the footpath a grand house, Wharfdale Hall, was built as a spa hotel in 1850.

Apart from the river, if there is one other consistent theme to this walk it is the stone. Right along the route, from Wetherby's bridge to these spa buildings, on to the houses of Tadcaster, and at York Minster itself, the same locally-quarried white and yellow magnesian limestone has been used.

Rather ominously, a couple of sandbags have been pressed up against the wooden gate to Wharfdale Hall, which suggests that the river – seemingly calm

and innocuous as it slides by, a good 10ft down the steep stone bank – may not have changed after all. So I'm not sorry when we part again, briefly, and I keep a close eye on it when we get back together at the hamlet of Newton Kyme.

On the riverbank here is a very fine house, Newton Kyme Hall, and a little church. On the approach the church's diminutive square tower looks a bit like Lego, but then appears pleasingly Saxon and rustic in profile, with its narrow windows placed high in the walls. In fact, Grade I-listed St Andrew's was built in the 12th century in pre-Conquest style.

Tadcaster

Today's final stretch, to Tadcaster, is the most bucolic of the walk. The Wharfe appears almost stationary as it glides in a series of leisurely turns through the meadows until, finally, a weir just before Tadcaster gets it all agitated again. So much so that, as it tumbles through this brewing town, it is beer-brown and acquires a head that the brewers at Sam Smith's, or its family rivals John Smith's, would be proud of.

Tadcaster is another old coaching town, and the ideal place for an overnight stop. I walk through the churchyard of St Mary's and into Kirkgate, where I pass a

Above: Sam Smith's – The Old Brewery

15

15th century timber-framed house called The Ark. Today it is council offices but it was once a non-conformist meeting house. It is said to have been used by the Pilgrim Fathers while they were planning their voyage to the New World and is named for the two carved figures on the exterior of Noah and his wife, Naamah.

You can't get away from beer in Tadcaster, so I don't try. There are regular whiffs of the mash tun in the High St, and a yeasty scent in the air, as if the whole place is just proving nicely, prior to being baked. For me, pilgrimage

Above: Barge on the Ouse, the river you follow into York. **Top**: Tadcaster weir and viaduct over the River Wharfe.

Above: Bishopthorpe Palace

and beer are inseparable, so I pop in to the Angel and White Horse, and am made replete.

The Roman road to York

After Tadcaster, the Wharfe and I finally separate, and I take up with a long stretch of Roman road, or rather the course of the road. It takes me in an almost unbroken line to within a few miles of York.

There is no sign of the old road now, and for miles the path is narrow, enclosed by thick hedges between arable fields, before breaking out to become a farm track, then looping over the modern A64 and taking to the fields again. I thread through the villages of Copmanthorpe and Bishopthorpe, where I take up with a new river: The Ouse.

Bishopthorpe Palace, which I pass just before reaching the Ouse, has been the residence of archbishops of York since the 13th century. It turns its back on the road, and its fair face to the river. I skirt the archbishop's grounds, with glimpses through the trees to his lake, on my way down to the riverbank where I turn upstream for the final approach to York. It is a great way to enter the city. Only when you are right in its heart do you have to leave the quiet riverbank and step up onto the roads.

York

Plenty of York's city walls remain intact, and you can walk them, but I suggest sticking to the pavements for now, as there are several places to see that are hard to reach directly from the walls' crenellated heights.

The first pilgrim point you encounter is the Bar Convent, at Micklegate, with its secret chapel hidden in the roof. This Catholic chapel dates from 1769, during the time when Catholicism was outlawed.

The sisters who run the Bar Convent, now also a guesthouse and heritage centre, belong to the religious community founded by Mary Ward in 1609. Ward wanted her sisters to be active in the community rather than hidden behind convent walls. Secretly, a convent and school were established in 1686. By 1766, they wanted a chapel – complete with a dome – but, as it was illegal to hear or celebrate Mass, such

Above: Micklegate, York

a building had to be disguised. A solution was found: it would be built in the attic, the dome hidden by a pitched tile roof.

Climbing a narrow staircase, you find an absolute Georgian gem: a mix of the elegant – with its white-painted, domed ceiling and graceful, gilded decoration – and the surreptitious. There is a priest hole hidden beneath the floor, and eight escape routes for the congregation. In a glass reliquary is the hand of a York martyr, St Margaret Clitherow, known as the 'Pearl of York'. Later we will visit her former home, now shrine, in The Shambles.

But first comes a site of vengeance against not Catholics, but Jews. In 1190, in a castle on the site now occupied by Clifford's Tower, York's entire Jewish population of around 150 was trapped by a mob. The Jews had fled here to seek protection during a period of increasing attacks upon them, but found themselves under siege. Realising they would all be murdered or, at the very least, forcibly baptised, they decided to die together. Fathers killed their wives and children, and then themselves. Before they died, they set fire to their possessions, and the wooden tower burned to the ground. It was among the very worst anti-Semitic atrocities of the Middle Ages. In the spring, daffodils flower on the mound around the tower, their six-pointed

Above: Bar Convent Chapel, York
Right: The Shambles

petals echoing the Star of David.

The Shambles, the narrow street that points towards York Minster, is now filled with shops selling Harry Potter and Lord of the Rings merchandise, but in one little house the true and very dark story of a saint is remembered. Margaret Clitherow, who was married to a prosperous butcher, became a Catholic in 1574. At a time when

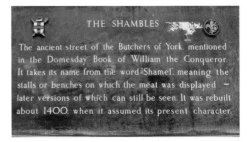

THE SHAMBLES

The ancient street of the Butchers of York, mentioned in the Domesday Book of William the Conqueror. It takes its name from the word 'Shamel', meaning the stalls or benches on which the meat was displayed – later versions of which can still be seen. It was rebuilt about 1400, when it assumed its present character.

15

it was an act of treason to be a Catholic priest in England, or to shelter a priest, Margaret had Mass celebrated here, above the shop. She also ran a small school to teach children the Catholic faith. She was betrayed and crushed to death between two doors on Good Friday 1586. There is a chapel now, in what was once the butcher's shop.

After so much that points to the evil performed in the name of faith, it is a relief to leave these dark places and enter the soaring, light-filled Minster. The vast nave, in that wonderful white and yellow magnesian limestone, lifts the spirit, as does the 15th century East Window, the largest expanse of medieval glass in England. And to climb the 275 steps of the central tower and look down at the medieval street pattern of York is truly awe inspiring.

YORK MINSTER AND ST WILLIAM

The first church on the site of today's York Minster was a wooden one built for the baptism of Edward, king of Northumbria.

His successor King Oswald built the first stone church, in 637, and dedicated it to St Peter, the apostle designated by Jesus as the rock upon which his church would be built.

When the murdered Thomas Becket was enshrined at Canterbury, that city became the major draw for pilgrims and their money, and York lost out. The greatest Christian city of the North needed a saint of its own, and petitioned Rome. In 1226 William Fitzherbert, a former Archbishop of York, was made St William of York by Pope Honorius. William may have been poisoned as part of a church feud but was not an obviously saintly figure, compared to Beckett with his credentials of martyrdom after defiance of a king, and it wasn't until 1279 that St William's remains were transferred to a shrine built for them behind the high altar.

St William never proved to be a big draw for pilgrims, and his veneration barely spread beyond York. His relics were lost for centuries but rediscovered in the 1960s and are now in the crypt.

Below: West Front, York Cathedral

16

The English Camino
Escomb to Finchale Priory via Durham

Walking from the unique Saxon church at Escomb, via Durham Cathedral and the shrines of St Cuthbert and St Oswald, to the home of St Godric the pilgrim pioneer at Finchale

The Wear will be my pilgrim guide, taking me all the way to Durham and beyond with barely the need to glance at a map. This path has been travelled by many pilgrims and at least one saint. St Godric, a 12th century hermit, is the first known English pilgrim to have travelled to St James's shrine at Santiago de Compostela, and a tradition emerged that to walk from Escomb via Durham to Finchale racked up credits when a pilgrim arrived in Spain.

How come? Because this route is part of the recognised English section of the Camino de Santiago, the *Camino Inglés*, which starts at the Spanish port cities of A Coruna and Ferrol, where medieval pilgrims traditionally arrived from England to continue their journey to St James's shrine.

The route had been forgotten for half a millennium until, in 2016, the Finchale Friends of the Camino was formed, and walked it once more. I should stress that my route differs from the official English Camino path, for which you would need more than two days. Instead my walk follows the Weardale Way while still taking in all the pilgrim points along the way. It does count for 25km towards the 100km required to have officially walked the Santiago Camino, and there is a Pilgrim Passport available in which to collect stamps as you go.

So, this walk is a perfect launch pad to ping you on to Santiago, but also lovely in itself. Along the way you encounter St Oswald, the warrior saint who Christianised the north, and visit his church, holy well and cathedral shrine at Durham. Also in the cathedral is the shrine of the other great northern saint, Cuthbert. Then it's back to the river for the final stretch to Finchale Priory, where the hermit Godric, pilgrim pioneer, lived for 50 years.

Durham Cathedral from the River Wear

16

PRACTICAL INFORMATION

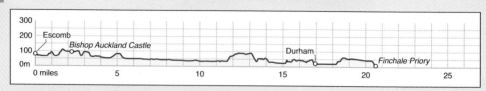

- **Terrain** Almost all well-maintained riverbank paths, short stretches on city streets
- **Difficulty** Easy
- **Directions & GPS*** 016.pdf, 016.gpx, 016.kml at 🖳 https://trailblazer-guides.com/press
  * See p10-11 for more information on downloads

ROUTE OVERVIEW   20.7 miles (33.3km)

Wonderfully peaceful riverside walking with a real sense of history along the route, and the added bonus of lovely views when the path climbs away from the river. Allow plenty of time to explore Durham Cathedral.

Escomb to Durham   16.7 miles (26.9km)

- **Time** 6 hours actual walking time   ● **Total ascent** 480m / 1575ft
- **Map** OS Explorer *305 Bishop Auckland; 308 Durham & Sunderland*

From Escomb church the route picks up the Weardale Way which is followed right to the final destination of Finchale. The walk runs alongside the River Wear, with a moderate climb, descent and a second climb, to reach Bishop Auckland in **2.2 miles**. It then crosses to the opposite bank for **9.2** miles to Sunderland Bridge, before leaving the river to ascend via Croxdale Hall **(0.5 miles)**. You descend through woodland back to the river, arriving at the outskirts of Durham in **3.9 miles** and Durham Cathedral in a further **0.9 miles**.

Durham to Finchale Priory   4 miles (6.4km)

- **Time** 1hr 40 mins actual walking time   ● **Total ascent** 120m / 395ft
- **Map** OS Explorer *308 Durham & Sunderland*

The route leaves the city centre alongside the River Wear, before a gentle climb along lanes and tarmacked paths and a final short, steep descent to Finchale Priory **(4 miles)**.

Day walk options

If you only have one day, end the walk at Durham, or for simpler access by public transport, start from Bishop Auckland. Alternatively start from Durham then walk to Finchale and back.

- **By public transport** The nearest station to Escomb is Bishop Auckland, a short taxi ride away. From Durham take a bus to Bishop Auckland or a longer taxi ride to Escomb.
- **Taxi** PTL Taxis (☎ 0191-3729961, 🖳 ptltaxis.co.uk)

PILGRIM PASSPORTS *Available from the Finchale Friends of the Camino, via their Facebook page, (Finchale Camino) or from the official Camino website (🖳 santiagode compostela.me)*

Where to eat or stay

● **Bishop Auckland Eat** lunch at *Breaking Bread Kitchen & Bakehouse* (formerly the Castlegate Café; (☎ 01388-608770; 🖥 face book.com/castlegatecafe, Mon-Sat 9am-4pm, 8 Market Place) for hearty walkers' food.

● **Durham Stay** in an apartment at *52 Old Elvet* (☎ 07504 954599; 🖥 52oldelvet.com), a Grade II listed mansion just across the river from the cathedral. **Eat** dinner at *Shaheens* (☎ 0191-3860960; 🖥 shaheensdurham.co.uk, 48 N Bailey), a cosy, family-run Indian curry house with the friendliest of staff; or splash out at *Marco Pierre White Steakhouse Bar and Grill* (☎ 0191-3293535; 🖥 mp wrestaurants.co.uk, 9 Old Elvet). Next morning enjoy veggie/vegan brunch at *Bean Social* (☎ 0191-3843378; 🖥 facebook.com/BeanSocialDurham, 24-28 N Rd).

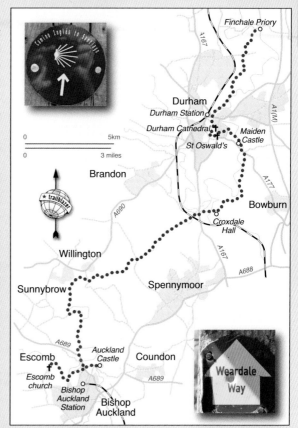

PILGRIMAGE HIGHLIGHTS

● Visit truly ancient places of worship: **Escomb Church** (🖥 escombsaxon church.co.uk, summer 9am-8pm, winter to 4pm; collect key at 28 Saxon Green, Escomb if locked) and **St Oswald's church** (🖥 oswalds.org.uk, 9am-5pm, Church St, Durham) with nearby **St Oswald's Well**.

● Explore **Auckland Castle**, the seat of many powerful bishops of Durham with **St Peter's chapel** (🖥 aucklandproject.org/st-peters-chapel).

● Attend Evensong at **Durham Cathedral** (🖥 durhamcathedral.co.uk; Evensong Tue-Sat 5.15pm Sun 3.30pm).

● Stroll along the riverbank to the atmospheric ruins of **Finchale Priory** (🖥 english-heritage.org.uk/visit/places/finchale-priory, open Apr-Oct 10am-5pm, Nov-March 10am-4pm, Framwellgate Moor), once home to the hermit St Godric, the first known English pilgrim to walk the Camino to Santiago.

Saints' days: St Cuthbert 20 March, St Godric 21 May, St Oswald 5 August

Above: Escomb Church.

Escomb church

We begin near the river, at Escomb, which has one of only three complete Saxon churches in England, and very possibly the oldest, dating from around 670. The church itself (**photo above**) is as stark and austere as I had expected, shaded by trees and enclosed by the high wall of a typically circular Saxon churchyard, yet its setting is jarringly modern. It sits on a traffic island on a little suburban road, encircled by a ring of squat modern houses. It was like finding a Leonardo propped up in a supermarket trolley.

But turn your back on the modern world around it and you have a church that is uncompromisingly Saxon: too tall and narrow to be in pleasing proportion; sombre, dark-stone walls; narrow arched windows set high; a rugged stone slate roof covered in a down of moss.

There is a 7th or 8th century sundial above the porch door and, inside, a Consecration cross cut into the stone, a Celtic device to show that the building had switched from a secular to religious use, and which links the building with the monks of St Cuthbert at Lindisfarne.

There are other signs of its heritage. A reused Roman stone with the markings LEG VI, referring to the sixth legion, set upside down in the north wall, and the

arch between the nave and chancel were probably taken from the Roman fort at nearby Binchester.

The church fell into ruin but was restored in the 1870s, and today is nurtured by those who live around it. But one other thing is curious, and I ponder the fact as I walk on towards Bishop Auckland, scrambling round a bend in the river where the Wear has undercut its bank, and the footpath. Escomb church has never taken on a saint's name. So it's an orphan, nameless and mysterious.

The pilgrim path climbs away from the river on the outskirts of Bishop Auckland and opens up a pleasing prospect: hills to either side, the river to look down upon, and an elegant stone viaduct – Newton Cap – stalking across the valley. It deserves a steam train puffing over it, but has to settle for a string of mundane cars and lorries.

Auckland Castle

Auckland Castle stands in an 800-acre deer park at the far end of this rather scuffed little town. For centuries it was home to the bishops of Durham and the present incumbent still has an office here. They lost it during the English Civil War, but won it back with the restoration of the monarchy, and embarked on extensive remodelling in which the banqueting hall was converted into a sumptuous chapel, dedicated to St Peter. It is still the bishop's private chapel, but is open for public services, and for pilgrims to collect a stamp on their pilgrim passports.

Among the castle's treasures is a set of twelve enormous canvases, *Jacob and his Twelve Sons* by the Spaniard Francisco de Zurbarán, bought in 1756 by Bishop Richard Trevor. The paintings relate to the passage in Genesis in which, as he lay

Above: Croxdale Viaduct.

dying, Jacob foretold the destiny of each son and their descendants, who founded the twelve tribes of Israel.

In February 2020 archaeologists rediscovered Bishop Bek's long-lost original chapel, built in around 1300 and one of the largest in Europe.

Is it just in contrast to the bustle of Bishop Auckland that the Wear seems calmer downstream from the town? No, it's definitely an older, more mature river now. A little wider, a little slower, with no desire to rush about like its adolescent, upstream self. The path parts from it for a while, and I walk up through the farms at Farnley Hill, then it's on through woods carpeted with deep purple bluebells, and down a wooded ridge to re-join the river, which slides past great slabs of rock, the path soft with strawberry-blonde sand. The afternoon is hot, the waters a deep and tempting bottle green.

Croxdale Hall & old St Bartholomew's
The going is cooler as I pass beneath the Croxdale Viaduct, cross the river and take the shady path up to Croxdale Hall. Beside

River Wear

Above: Old St Bartholomew's church and the Tree of Life carving (**right**).

the house, home to the Catholic Salvin family since 1402, is a 12th century church that I would dearly love to visit, but can't.

Once this was the local parish church for the nearby village of Sunderland Bridge, and the Salvins built their own Gothic Revival chapel in their house in 1807, although Catholic worship was still outlawed. Then in 1845 the church was sold to the Salvins in exchange for the land to build a new parish church, St Bartholomew's, down in the village. The old church became a family chapel, and the churchyard the family burial ground. Yet today the church is shut up, its windows milky cataracts, and is on English Heritage's Buildings at Risk register.

I have to make do with leaning over the churchyard gate, admiring the original Norman oak door, above which a crumbling sandstone tympanum faintly shows a relief carving of the Tree of Life. There are various interpretations of what the Tree of Life means. In Genesis it is the source of eternal life in the Garden of Eden. In the Book of Revelation it appears as part of the new garden of paradise, no longer forbidden to the faithful. Augustine of Hippo said that the Tree of Life is Christ himself, and in Eastern Christianity it is the love of God. Me, I'll take comfort in all of those.

The approach to Durham

From here the path follows the lip of a steep, thickly wooded drop to the river, before slaloming down through the trees (**photo left**) to the river. There is such a lush crop of bright, white-flowering wild garlic here in the gloom that it's as if the ground is lit by stars. The smell is like tucking in to *gambas al ajillo* with garlic bread and extra garlic butter.

The path slips you in by the back door to Durham. Skirting the promi-

nent wooded mound of Maiden Castle, it leaves the river to climb up through suburban streets and skirt Durham Prison, where my first glimpse of the cathedral is through a roll of razor wire topping a wall.

St Oswald's church and Well

It's quiet, as if the city is sleeping. I can't think of a better approach to a city or, indeed, a better city. Then comes the oasis of St Oswald's churchyard. The dedication to this 7th century king of Northumbria, the original round shape of the churchyard, and the Anglo-Saxon sculpted stones in the walls of St Oswald's are all clues pointing to a very ancient place of worship.

Top: Durham Castle and Framwellgate Bridge.
Above: Durham Cathedral from Palace Green.

Taking the path from the far side of the churchyard you descend and find St Oswald's Well, hidden away in a cavern cut into the sandstone to your left, its waters running beneath the path to tumble into the River Wear. The river loops in an oxbow around the city centre, shielding its cathedral and castle like a moat. Rock cliffs rise sheer from its banks, and you see what a natural fortress this place was.

I pass over Prebend Bridge and into the inner sanctum. The cathedral has been towering above me for some way now, but to turn the corner and come smack up against it is still awe inspiring.

Durham Cathedral

I skirt round the tourists and pass inside. The great pillars in the nave, the dark stone, the rose window. I'm lost, until a guide points out that they are about to close, unless I'm here for evensong? I find that I am, and am ushered through to a seat just before the choir, where I am told to wait. A scattering of others join me, and a hunched figure in a black cloak shuffles over to a braided rope, which he pulls. Far away, a deep chime resonates. He pulls again.

For 10 minutes the chimes ring out, then we are beckoned through into the choir itself and ushered into the very stalls alongside those the choristers will occupy in a moment. This is such a hallowed place, I'm quite transported. The red-gowned (visiting) choir file to their places,

DURHAM AND ST CUTHBERT

St Cuthbert's relics came to Durham in a roundabout way. Cuthbert was a bishop who became a hermit and settled on Holy Island, Lindisfarne. He was declared a saint in 698. The Lindisfarne part of his story is covered in Walk 19, but when a Viking invasion in 793 forced the monks to flee Holy Island, they took Cuthbert's remains with them. They were carried around the north of England before the monks, and Cuthbert, found a final resting place at Durham. The present cathedral stands on the site of the original Anglo-Saxon church which contained his shrine.

In 1104 a new shrine, fabulously decorated with jewels and semi-precious stones, was built in the new Norman cathedral, and became a hugely important pilgrim destination in the Middle Ages. That shrine was destroyed at the reformation, to be replaced in 1542 with a simple marble slab (**photo left**) marked *Cuthbertus* and surrounded by stones from the smashed shrine.

then comes the deep resonance of the great organ, and those pure, soaring, exultant voices.

Afterwards, my head buzzing as if great cymbals have been clapped beside my ears, I weave my unsteady way into the ordinary world.

Next morning I return to take in the rest of the treasures in this remarkable place. St Cuthbert's Tomb, a simple polished granite stone, is flanked by the headless statue of St Cuthbert, holding the head of St Oswald, which was reputedly buried along with his remains. In the 14th century Great Kitchen are displayed St Cuthbert's original 7th century wooden coffin, his gold and garnet pectoral cross, the portable altar and ivory comb placed in his coffin when he was buried, and richly embroidered Anglo-Saxon vestments

I leave the city centre by another bridge, Framwellgate, and climb down to

the riverbank for the walk north to Finchale. This is a very popular Sunday afternoon walk and cycle route, and the path is busy for the first time since leaving Bishop Auckland as my way leaves the Wear, climbs steadily through fields and woods, skirts another prison – Frankland – before dropping me suddenly down to my final destination: Finchale Priory.

Durham Cathedral clock.

Finchale Priory

Finchale may have been austere when St Godric was here, but today it is a place for ice creams and riverside picnics. Although it has none of the solitude Godric sought, it is still a spot of un-

Above: Finchale Priory.

deniable beauty, the river wide and benign, the rock banks making paddling a simple pleasure. The monks of Durham certainly thought it was a place to enjoy. The priory founded here in 1196 on the site of Godric's hermitage became a holiday retreat for them until its suppression in 1538. You can still trace the priory's story in the remains, from Godric's original chapel, his tomb and its centuries as a priory. I spent a lazy time wandering the ruins, and lounging on the riverbank, before popping into the tearoom to stamp my *Camino Ingles* passport and establish my claim to being a quarter of the way to Santiago de Compostela.

Godric, according to his biographer, the monk Reginald of Durham, was a poor itinerant pedlar who became a seaman and merchant. He combined his voyages with pilgrimage, reaching Jerusalem in 1102 and, on his way back, visiting Santiago de Compostela.

In about 1104 he abandoned the sea and became a hermit, living in caves and woods with another hermit at Wolsingham in upper Weardale, but making at least one further pilgrimage to Jerusalem.

A few years later, the Bishop of Durham allowed him to settle on church-owned land where Finchale Priory's ruins now stand. For the last 50 years of his life he lived here, in a turf-roofed hut alongside a simple chapel. His regime was austere. He fasted regularly, slept on a stone pillow, and bathed in the often-freezing waters of the Wear, or in a barrel sunk into the floor of the chapel.

Despite living in such isolation he became famous, and was visited by Thomas Becket, Pope Alexander III and William the Lion, king of Scotland. He died, aged around 100, on 21 May 1170. He was buried in his chapel, the spot now marked by a cross in the grass.

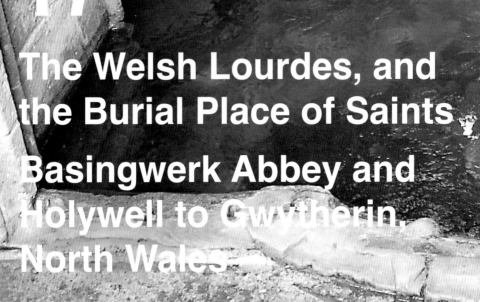

17

The Welsh Lourdes, and the Burial Place of Saints

Basingwerk Abbey and Holywell to Gwytherin, North Wales

Following in the footsteps of St Winefride, from her holy well and shrine at Holywell, through rolling hills and valleys to the place where she ended her days

The waters of St Winefride's Well never waver from an icy 10°C, and to plunge in fully clothed can take your breath away, even on a sunny day like this. Yet the pilgrims are not deterred. As I sit on a bench at a little distance from the bathing pool that is fed by the well, a family slip, one by one, beneath the guard chains and into the chill waters.

I have been to many pilgrim sites, but never found one at which the veneration so clearly follows the ancient tradition. For 13 centuries this well in the little north Wales town of Holywell has been a pilgrim destination. Apart from the Dorset parish church at Whitchurch Canonicorum (see Walk 5) it is the only shrine in Britain of which this can be said. For all those centuries, the rituals will have been performed here, exactly as I see them today.

Once they have entered the 3ft deep waters, pilgrims follow the tradition of walking three times around the pool, then kneel on a stone and kiss a cross cut into the bath's edge. This group is a big, extended family from Ireland, and first parents, then grandparents and finally children slip into the waters. Even the babies have their heads dipped.

Medieval pilgrims will have walked here, as I have, up the narrow, steep-sided valley from Basingwerk Abbey, close to where the boats landed them on the banks of the River Dee. The abbey there, whose ruins now slumber in the sun, welcomed and refreshed them.

They came, then as now, because of a 7th century saint called Winefride – Gwenfrewi in Welsh – and this walk traces her life story. From Holywell, it will take me over the rolling hills and valleys to the village of Gwytherin, where Winefride founded a monastery, and died. In Gwytherin, she had chosen a site of veneration stretching back to pre-Christian times, and the burial place of Welsh kings, queens and saints.

Along the way, the route touches many pilgrim places, piggy-backing for the first stretch from Basingwerk to Pantasaph on the North Wales Pilgrim's Way long-distance path. You can buy a Pilgrim Passport at both Basingwerk and Holywell, and collect stamps at all the pilgrim points along this walk.

Holywell – St Winefride's Well

PRACTICAL INFORMATION

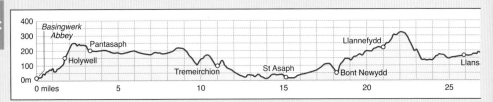

- **Terrain** Wide range of footpaths and lanes; frequent, sustained ascents and descents.
- **Difficulty** Challenging (particularly on the two-day option)
- **Directions & GPS*** 017.pdf, 017.gpx, 017.kml at 🖳 https://trailblazer-guides.com/press
  * See p10-11 for more information on downloads

ROUTE OVERVIEW   33 miles (53.1km)

This slightly longer pilgrimage is best spread across three days to give you time to enjoy the pilgrim highlights along the way, but if you're up for a challenge it can also be done in two days.

Three-day option

Basingwerk Abbey to St Asaph   15 miles (24.1km)
- **Time** 6hrs 45 mins actual walking time
- **Total ascent** 687m/2254ft
- **Map** OS Explorer *265 Clwydian Range, 264 Vale of Clwyd*

From Basingwerk Abbey, follow the Celtic cross markers of the North Wales Pilgrim's Way for **1.1 miles** to Holywell, and on to climb over rough pasture, via the summit of Pen-y-Ball, for **3 miles** to Pantasaph. You then leave the Pilgrim's Way along quiet lanes for **6.6 miles** to the outskirts of Rhuallt. From here, follow a path across meadows to climb, then descend to reach Tremeirchion, after **1.5 miles**, before taking lanes and paths over level meadows for **4 miles** to St Asaph.

St Asaph to Llansannan   10.7 miles (17.2km)
- **Time** 4hrs 35mins actual walking time
- **Total ascent** 725m/2378ft
- **Map** OS Explorer *264 Vale of Clwyd*

Pick up the North Wales Pilgrim's Way on quiet lanes out of St Asaph for **3 miles** to Bont-Newydd, then on over gently undulating country for **2.8 miles** to Llannefydd, leaving it shortly before the village. After Llannefydd you initially follow lanes, then the valley of the River Aled, for **4.7 miles** to Llansannan before returning to the Pilgrim's Way just after Bryn Rhyd-yr-Arian.

Llansannan to Gwytherin   7.3 miles (11.8km)

- **Time** 2hrs actual walking time
- **Total ascent** 197m / 646ft

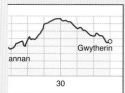

- **Map** OS Explorer *264 Vale of Clwyd & OL17 Snowdon*

Today's much shorter walk takes the North Wales Pilgrim's Way all the way to Gwytherin. The route runs along the Aled Valley for **3 miles**, before climbing steeply and crossing high moorland for **3.5 miles,** followed by the final descent via a lane to Gwytherin.

Two-day option
Basingwerk to Llannefydd   21 miles (33.8km)
- **Time** 9hrs 45mins actual walking time   • **Total ascent** 1202m / 3943ft
- **Map** OS Explorer *265 Clwydian Range, 264 Vale of Clwyd*

Llannefydd to Gwytherin   12 miles (19.3km)
- **Time** 3hrs 45mins actual walking time   • **Total ascent** 407m / 1335ft
- **Map** OS Explorer *264 Vale of Clwyd & OL17 Snowdon*

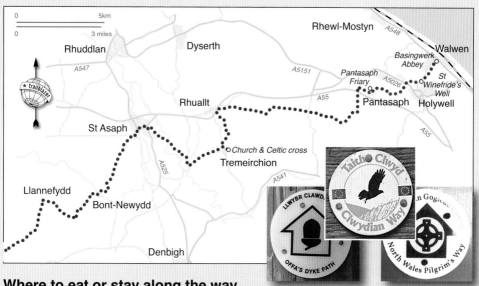

Where to eat or stay along the way
- **Holywell** For a true pilgrim experience **stay** at *St Winefride's Guest House* (☎ 01352-714172, ⌨ bridgettine.org, 20 New Rd), formerly the Pilgrims' Hospice, now run by the Bridgettine Sisters.
- **Tremeirchion** Stop for lunch at the *Salusbury Arms* (☎ 01745-710532; from noon).
- **St Asaph** *Talardy Hotel* (☎ 01745-799314, ⌨ talardyhotelstasaph.co.uk, noon-10pm).
- **Llannefydd** *Hawk and Buckle* (☎ 01745-540249, ⌨ thehawkandbuckle.com; Wed-Sun from 6pm, food 6pm-8pm).
- **Llansannan** *Red Lion* (☎ 01745-870256, ⌨ facebook.com / redlionllansannan).

PILGRIMAGE HIGHLIGHTS

● **Visit Basingwerk Abbey** (🖥 cadw.gov.wales/visit/places-to-visit/basingwerk-abbey; 10am-4pm) and **St Winefride's Shrine, Holywell** (🖥 saintwinefrideswell.com; Mon-Sat 10am-3.30pm, Sun 11am-3pm, Greenfield St). Pick up your **Pilgrim Passport** at either of the above and have it stamped at pilgrim points along the way.
● **Walk** the Stations of the Cross at **Pantasaph Friary** (🖥 pantasaph.org.uk; 10am-4pm, Monastery Rd).
● Complete your journey at the former **St Winefride's** church in **Gwytherin** (🖥 thegwenfrewiproject.co.uk) and **explore** the burial place of Welsh kings, queens and saints.

St Winefride's Saint's Day: 22 June.
National Catholic Pilgrimage to Holywell, the Sunday after the saint's day.

Basingwerk Abbey to Holywell

From Basingwerk the path climbs the narrow, steep-sided Greenfield Valley up through woods to Holywell. The Holywell stream, fed by the holy well I am headed for, tumbles beside the path, falling over the weirs and dams that are the remnants of industry. In the 13th century the monks harnessed the power of this river to run a corn mill, and to treat the wool from their sheep, beginning centuries of industrial exploitation.

St Winefride's Well and Shrine

When I emerge at the top of the valley, and reach the shrine on the outskirts of Holywell, I am moved by both the physical and spiritual power of this water.

Above: The ruins of Basingwerk Abbey.

Above: *The Miracle*, a 4m stainless steel sculpture unveiled in Holywell town in 2014.

Every minute, 3000 gallons surge up through the 7ft deep, bottle green waters of the well basin, which is enclosed in a traceried canopy, forming a crypt. Above the crypt is a 16th century chapel. They were built – probably partly through the munificence of Henry VII's mother, Lady Margaret Beaufort – by the Cistercian monks of Basingwerk, to replace an earlier building. Henry is said to have made a secret visit here before winning his crown at Bosworth in 1485.

Richard III was an earlier royal patron, and Henry V made the pilgrimage here in 1415 after his victory at Agincourt. In 1605, many of those soon to be involved with the Gunpowder Plot came with Edward Oldcorne, a Jesuit priest, to give thanks for having his throat cancer cured after a previous visit or, as some have it, to plan the plot.

In the shrine's little museum are piles of walking sticks discarded by those who have believed themselves cured. The walls of the shrine are graffitied with names and dates of their deliverance from their affliction. Today, many who don't go to the extent of bathing fill a bottle.

Below: St Winefride's Well

Holywell to Pantasaph Friary

The climb gets steeper after Holywell and the path more rugged, but with stunning views back across the River Dee to Birkenhead. At Pen-y-Ball a second vista opens up, to your left, of the Halkyn Mountain, and the hills to the south. The heights scaled, for now at least, the path winds around a disused stone quarry and through a thicket of

THE STORY OF ST WINEFRIDE, HOLYWELL AND GWYTHERIN

According to legend, in 660 St Winefride was the victim of an attempted rape by Caradog, the son of a prince, and when she resisted he cut off her head with his sword. The well is said to have erupted at the spot where her head came to rest. But Winefride was restored to life through the prayers of her uncle St Beuno, and she lived as a nun until her second death, 22 years later. Whatever the truth of the legend, Winefride and Beuno did exist.

For believers, St Winefride is a sort of Welsh Lazarus who pointed towards the resurrection of Jesus, and to the eventual resurrection of all who believe in Him. If you think this all sounds like magical realism, you are not alone. The author Ellis Peters used the story of St Winefride in *A Morbid Taste for Bones*, the first in her series of medieval mysteries, *The Cadfael Chronicles*. Much of the book is set in Gwytherin.

St Winefride and St Beuno

aromatic gorse to Pantasaph.

Pantasaph Friary is quite a place. The Franciscan friars who created it in 1847 intended it to be 'a light on a hill'; a place of prayer, reflection and solace, and it still feels like a blessed oasis for pilgrims passing through this rugged country. There is St David's church, which owes

Pantasaph Friary – top: Pugin designs on the walls and **(above)** stations of the cross on the Woodland Walk.

its remarkably rich ornamentation, with walls stencilled in vivid red, blue and green, to AWN Pugin (See Walk 1), and a garden shrine to St Padre Pio, the Franciscan saint who bore the marks of Christ's crucifixion – the stigmata – for most of his life. But what I love the most is the woodland walk alongside the Stations of the Cross. Fourteen scenes depict key points on Christ's final journey to crucifixion, with each of the gated stations like a mini shrine in itself. The walk leads uphill to a clearing in which are erected three crosses: a life-sized representation of Calvary. There is a

café here, and a shop where you can have your pilgrim passport stamped.

Pantasaph to Tremeirchion

After Pantasaph I leave the North Wales Pilgrim's Way, and take to the lanes to the outskirts of the village of Rhuallt. From Rhuallt, briefly following the course of the Offa's Dyke Path, I climb through meadows full of buttercups and clover to Maen Efa. The views up here are wonderful: the long low coastline to my right where the River Clwyd reaches the sea at Rhyll; ahead of me the Vale of Clwyd and St Asaph, with Denbigh to my left.

On my right as I pass through woods, on my way to the village of Tremeirchion and lunch, is St Beuno's College. Once a seminary, and attended by the poet Gerard Manley Hopkins, it is now a Jesuit Spirituality Centre running silent retreats. The actors Andrew Garfield and Adam

Above: Views of the distant peaks of Snowdonia National Park as you approach Gwytherin.

Driver attended a retreat here while preparing for roles in Martin Scorsese's 2016 film *Silence*.

Tremeirchion

There is a curious connection between St Beuno's College and the Anglican church of Corpus Christi in Tremeirchion. In 1862 the college was given a 14th century stone Celtic cross called the Tremeirchion Rood of Grace. The head of this cross had lain in the grass of the churchyard ever since being smashed off its shaft by Oliver Cromwell's men. An archaeologist spotted it, bought it from the churchwarden for five sovereigns and offered it to St Beuno's to look after. In 2004 St Beuno's returned it to the church, and it was restored to its old place beneath a yew in the churchyard.

The cross was a popular shrine for medieval pilgrims and became known as the Miracle Cross. Three hundred years after it was desecrated, it is again an important

shrine for pilgrims. I sit at its foot in the sun, admiring the simplicity of the partly 12th century stone and slate church, which might be mistaken for a cottage if not for the cross on one gable and the bell on the other. Christian worship at this site may date back to the 7th century, and the first church established by St Beuno.

Equally sustaining for a hungry, thirsty pilgrim is the Salusbury Arms, next door.

Tremeirchion to St Asaph

The walk begins along quiet lanes via Bryn Ibod and then over a stone-slab stile for the cross-country approach to St Asaph, the path running alongside Dormitory Wood and then across meadows dotted with mighty oaks and crowded with sheep. The path picks up signs for both the Clwydian Way and North Wales Pilgrim's Way for the last stretch to St Asaph, then drops down to the bed of the long-disused Vale of Clwyd railway line to reach the city.

Below: Tremeirchion Church and (**inset**) the Tremeirchion Rood of Grace.

Above: The current St Asaph bridge was built in 1770 to replace the earlier wooden structure.

St Asaph

St Asaph is a cathedral city the size of a village. Its name in Welsh – Llanelwy – translates as 'the sacred religious enclosure'. The cathedral stands on a square plot at the top of the descent to the River Elwy, embraced by the streets of little shops. St Asaph may be small, but it bustles, and has huge historic significance. A church was founded here by St Kentigern in around 550 and his disciple Asaph took over when he left. The first cathedral was built in 1152.

When Latin was banned for church services at the Reformation, the Welsh language was also outlawed. But, in 1588, William Morgan translated the Bible into Welsh here. A russet stone memorial pillar (**photo right**) in the cathedral grounds marks that achievement, and a copy of the first Welsh Bible is on display in the cathedral. I slip inside to find the choir rehearsing, and stamp my pilgrim passport while I wait for choral evensong to begin.

St Asaph to Llannefydd

Next morning I descend the high street and cross the River Elwy, still on the North Wales Pilgrim's Way, to walk quiet lanes before dipping down to rejoin the Elwy in the narrow valley at Bont-Newydd.

The hamlet is just a nip and tuck in the road, a few houses, all surrounded, of course, by thousands of sheep. Two farmers are having a conversation in Welsh from either side of the valley, its high sides bouncing their words between them, then sending them echoing off down the valley.

The route follows the valley upstream from Bont-Newydd before angling off to climb through a pine plantation and then over pasture. An old green way that clearly doubles as a river bed in wet weather takes me to lanes so narrow and worn they threatened to crumble back into footpaths before the approach to Llannefydd.

Llannefydd

The church of St Nefydd & St Mary boasts that 'Katheryn of Berain, known as the Mother of Wales, is buried in this church'. Katheryn, a 16th century noblewoman and direct descendant of Henry VII, earned the title thanks to her many children, fathered by four husbands.

Above: Llannefydd – pub and church.

The beautifully restored 17th Century coaching inn, The Hawk and Buckle, makes a perfect overnight stop here.

Llannefydd to Llansannan

I leave by the narrow lane opposite the pub, which takes me up to the top of the world. At Pen-y-Bryn there are spectacular views ahead along the Aled Valley. That's Aled as in 'poet', the valley having been home to several prominent Welsh-language bards from the 15th to 19th centuries. The path leaves the lane to skirt the hillside, taking you obliquely and gently down into the valley, walking right into that mesmerising view.

Llansannan

Llansannan is another welcoming village, with the Red Lion Inn being a good second-night stop on a three-day walk. There is a pilgrim passport stamp in the church of St Sannan. It's only 7.5 miles from here to Gwytherin, which means a leisurely morning's walk and plenty of time to enjoy the remarkable culmination of this pilgrimage.

I continue along the Aled Valley next morning. There are some fine waterfalls along the way, the water tumbling over high-stacked strata of rock. To my right, each field on the hillside is a subtly different shade of green, as if a great colour chart has been spread out in the sun.

At Rhyd-loew, the farmhouse roof is staved in as if a giant's boot has stamped on it, and the pillars supporting the footbridge over the river have been knocked off kilter by tree trunks sent smashing into them during a flood. I cross this wonky bridge carefully, then climb up to the moors. Up here it is very different from the lush Aled Valley. The patchwork of field is replaced with an expanse of sun-scorched grass, and the views are of the grey-purple peaks of the Snowdonia National Park.

GWYTHERIN – THE BURIAL PLACE OF SAINTS

Gwytherin was a holy place long before Winefride made it her home. As you walk through the churchyard of the now-deconsecrated 19th century St Winefride's chapel, a line of four standing stones (**photo, right**) dating from the Bronze Age – 3000 to 1200 BC – leads you on to three yews that are between 2500 and 3000 years old. These impressive yews indicate an ancient, sacred gathering place.

Several other Welsh holy figures were laid to rest here, in what became known as The Burial Place of Saints. They include St Cybi, cousin of St David; St Eleri, prince, abbot and cousin of St Winefride; his mother Theonia; and St Sannan, a friend of Winefride's father. The village of Llansannan, which you passed through earlier, derives its name from him.

Early Christians believed that the burial place of a saint provided spiritual protection to a community, hence Gwytherin became one of the best-protected and most holy places in Wales.

Gwytherin

Hidden in a fold in the hills is the hamlet of Gwytherin, the natural conclusion in the story of St Winefride. To the south of the present churchyard is a mound on which Winefride's original chapel, Capel Gwenfrewi, once stood. It was built over her open grave, and afflicted pilgrims would come and sleep in the grave in hope of a cure. In the 11th century, after a

The burial place of Welsh kings, queens and saints, Gwytherin.

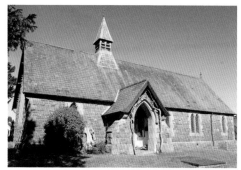

Above: Former chapel of St Winefride, Gwytherin, and the ancient standing stone beside it.

sick monk from Shrewsbury who had bathed at her well at Holywell was cured, the reliquary that held Winefride's remains was exhumed and taken to Shrewsbury Cathedral. This was a blatant hijacking, designed to divert Winefride's power, and force the many pilgrims who sought to venerate her to begin their journey to Holywell, and Gwytherin, from Shrewsbury.

An elaborately carved wooden chest that once encased the reliquary remained in Capel Gwenfrewi until the 18th century, but so many pilgrims took fragments from it that virtually nothing was left. The chapel was converted into a cottage and later demolished, and the graveyard dug up.

St Winefride's power, diminished for periods, has always proved resurgent. In 1896 the current chapel was built. In 2004, it was deconsecrated and abandoned but, five years on, it found a saviour in Alison Goulbourne (**below**), a musician and artist. She restored the building, and founded the Gwenfrewi project to use the church as a historic centre, for civil weddings and to spread the word about St Winefride.

18

St Hilda, Blessed Nicholas Postgate and the first English poet

Danby to Whitby, North Yorkshire

Walking the Esk Valley on the trail of a saint, the martyred priest of the moors, and the shepherd who praised God in one of the oldest surviving pieces of English poetry

An ancient packhorse route wends its narrow way down the Esk Valley to Whitby. Its centuries old stones, great lozenges of granite worn concave by countless feet and hooves, snake on ahead of you: crossing meadows, following field margins, running through woods, stepping up hills, fording rivers.

For mile after mile it points the way, no wider than a garden path. Sometimes you lose it, but then it appears again. This is the route that took Caedmon, the first English poet, to the sanctuary that St Hilda offered at her priory high on the cliffs above Whitby. It is among the paths used by the Catholic martyr Nicholas Postgate, the fugitive priest of the moors, to flit from safe house to safe house. And, among the many villagers, merchants and farmers who used it every day, would have come a steady stream of pilgrims. How blessed to be able to follow it as a pilgrim today.

I pick up the path at Glaisdale, but my pilgrimage begins further up the valley when I hop off the Esk Valley Railway at Danby.

Danby Castle

PRACTICAL INFORMATION

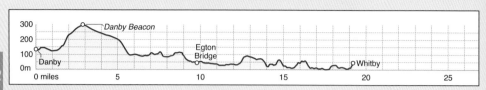

- **Terrain** Mainly well-maintained paths over grass, rough-paved packhorse routes, and farm tracks.
- **Difficulty** Moderate
- **Directions & GPS*** 018.pdf, 018.gpx, 018.kml at 🖳 https://trailblazer-guides.com/press

* See p10-11 for more information on downloads

ROUTE OVERVIEW   19.3 miles (31.1km)

Although there is a fair bit of up and down on this walk, the views more than make up for the effort involved. The Esk Valley Railway (🖳 eskvalleyrailway.co.uk) shadows the route, meaning you could access the start at Danby by train from Whitby, or choose other start and end points along the way.

Danby to Egton Bridge   9.9 miles (16km)

- **Time** 4hrs 30mins actual walking time
- **Total ascent** 610m/2001ft
- **Map** OS Explorer *OL27 North York Moors Eastern Area*

The route follows the Esk Valley Walk throughout, its roundels depicting a black salmon against a yellow arrow, and it is reasonably well signposted. Shortly after Danby, the route climbs steeply out of the valley onto the moors, reaching Danby Beacon in **2.7 miles,** before descending gently to Lealholm **(2.7 miles)** then running close to the River Esk, reaching Egton Bridge in a further **4.5 miles**.

Egton Bridge to Whitby   9.4 miles (15.1km)

- **Time** 4hrs 15 mins actual walking time
- **Total ascent** 218m/715ft
- **Map** OS Explorer *OL27 North York Moors Eastern Area*

Today's walk is gentle until the very end, following the river via Sleights **(5.2 miles)** and Ruswarp **(2.1 miles)**, reaching the centre of Whitby in **1.6 miles**, before the climb up 199 steps to Whitby Abbey, reached after a further **0.5 mile**.

Day walk options

The Esk Valley Railway shadows this route, meaning you can start and end at several different points along the way (🖳 eskvalleyrailway.co.uk).

- **By public transport** The Esk Valley Railway connects Middlesborough and Whitby. Along the course of this walk there are stops at Danby, Lealholm, Glaisdale, Egton, Grosmont, Sleights & Ruswarp.

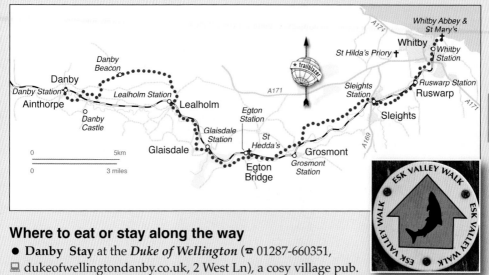

Where to eat or stay along the way

● **Danby** **Stay** at the *Duke of Wellington* (☎ 01287-660351, 🖥 dukeofwellingtondanby.co.uk, 2 West Ln), a cosy village pub.

● **Egton Bridge** **Stay at** *The Postgate* (☎ 01947-895241, 🖥 postgateinn.com; food from 6pm) a friendly country inn and restaurant with hearty food.

● **Whitby Stay** at *The Belfry* (☎ 01947-600860, 🖥 thebelfrywhitby.co.uk, 2 Church Sq) a boutique family-run B&B with great Yorkshire breakfasts. **Eat** fine fish and chips at family-run *Hadley's* (☎ 01947-604153, 🖥 hadleysfishandchips.co.uk; Sun-Thur 11am-7.30pm, Fri & Sat 11am-8.30pm) at 11 Bridge St.

PILGRIMAGE HIGHLIGHTS

● **Views** all the way to the coast from Danby Beacon and from atmospheric Whitby Abbey.

● Attend Mass (Sun 9.30am) at **St Hedda's, Egton Bridge** (🖥 middlesbrough-diocese.org.uk/parishes/st-hedda-egton-bridge) with its stained-glass window portraying Blessed Nicholas Postgate and collection of mementoes of the man.

● Visit **St Mary's** church, **Whitby** (🖥 achurchnearyou.com/church/19387; 11am-3.30pm, Abbey Plain) with its cross telling the story of Caedmon, the first English poet, and **Whitby Abbey** (🖥 english-heritage.org.uk/visit/places/whitby-abbey, Apr-Sept 10am-6pm, Oct-Nov 10am-5pm) to learn about St Hilda and the legend of the headless stone snakes.

St Hilda's feast day: 17 November (Roman Catholic church), 19 November (C of E).
Nicholas Postgate Rally: First Sunday in July, venue Egton Bridge (2021),
Ugborough (2022) and alternating from there.

Danby

Danby is among a string of villages hunkered down along The Esk Valley, which runs like a green river through the brown moors. The riverside meadows have just been cut for hay as I pick up the Esk Valley Walk, which I shall follow all the way to Whitby. It has been raked into long straight heaps to dry before it is gathered, and field after field bears a pattern like a head of braided hair. The grass gives off a fresh, sweet scent this grey Yorkshire morning.

I reach the banks of the River Esk which is meandering aimlessly, forming a series of pools in which the water turns lazily, as if it has no particular place to go, before rolling over a rocky shallow ridge into the next pool. A heron stands silently by one of the shallow stretches, watching for fish as they slide from one pool of safety to the next, but he seems distracted, as if his heart isn't really in the hunt.

Path, river and railway run in a plait along the valley floor, weaving around each other as they will right down the

Above: Stone slabs on the old packhorse route through the Esk valley.
Below: Lealholm Moor.

valley, apart from the next stretch over Danby Beacon. The Esk is one of Yorkshire's finest salmon and sea trout rivers, and a salmon appears on the signs for the Esk Valley Walk.

Lealholm Moor and Danby Beacon

As I leave the valley for the moors and the gradient steepens, I hunch forward. I pass through a farm where a couple of calves are skittering around free in the yard in a bovine game of tag.

With height I get to survey the valley, and look across to see, on a moorland spur, a substantial stone building that could be a ruined monastery, but in fact is 14th century Danby Castle. It has a curious connection with pilgrimage.

In the 16th century it was owned by John Neville, Lord Latimer, who held the office of gentleman-pensioner (bodyguard) to Henry VIII. When, at the Reformation, the northern nobles rebelled against Henry's Dissolution of the Monasteries, and marched south in what became known as the Pilgrimage of Grace, Neville

got caught up in the rebellion, possibly being captured by the rebels rather than embracing their cause voluntarily. He said of the episode: 'My being among them was a very painful and dangerous time to me'. However, he represented the rebels at peace talks in 1536 and helped negotiate an amnesty, which was later betrayed. Neville was married to Catherine Parr who, after his death, became Henry VIII's sixth wife.

I watch the white worm of the train to Whitby buzz through beneath me and turn to the serious business of reaching the top. Pushing up through the heather is a great smooth egg of rock, like a cartoon bump on the head poking through brown hair.

The moor is alive with birdsong, and a sign warns that this – March to July – is the peak time for upland nesting birds. They are territorial and send up guards to watch me on my way. I spot red grouse, perfectly camouflaged except for the red stop light on top of the head, and black grouse with white wing bars and shoulder patches. Some birds I can't see, but I can certainly hear their alarm calls. What a cacophony.

At the summit of the moor is Danby Beacon, and a brief glimpse of the sea, 10 miles away at Whitby. All around is blasted heath, but I can trace some of the route I shall take along the green Esk Valley. There has been a beacon here since the 1600s, to be lit as a warning should French warships approach the coast.

As I begin the long slow descent to Lealholm I find, at a junction of several tracks, two cut stones that are the remnants of an old cross. Maybe it was just a waypost for those trekking from dale to dale, but I wonder if this could also have marked a preaching spot for Nicholas Postgate, the 17th century fugitive priest who slipped from place to place saying Mass while Catholicism was outlawed, and whose story I would learn more about at Egton Bridge, my overnight stop.

Below: Fording the river near Underpark.

THE BLESSED NICHOLAS POSTGATE

Catholicism flourished in Yorkshire in the 17th century, despite being forced underground by the severe penalties imposed on those who refused to renounce the old faith and attend an Anglican service each week. In the Esk Valley, the support of local Catholic gentry enabled Nicholas Postgate to carry out surreptitious baptisms, weddings and funerals, and say Mass at secret churches hidden in safe houses, or out on the moors.

Postgate, who was born in Egton Bridge, trained for the priesthood in the Douai seminary in what was then the Spanish Netherlands, now France, before being smuggled back, perhaps by Whitby fishermen, to serve a secret parish that stretched between Pickering, Guisborough and Scarborough. He carried a portable altar stone like a schoolroom writing slate, and a communion chalice that divided into three parts to disguise its purpose.

Many priests followed the same mission, but they lasted an average of only six months. Postgate survived for 49 years, until he was betrayed and arrested in the act of baptism. He was hanged, drawn and quartered in York at the age of 83.

Postgate was beatified in 1987 – hence the appellation Blessed – setting him on the road to sainthood. Many families in the villages on this pilgrimage are de-

scended from Postgate's parishioners, and his legacy is cherished in the Esk Valley.

A hymn he wrote includes these haunting lines:

'And thus dear Lord, I fly about
In weak and weary case,
And like the dove that Noah sent out
I find no resting-place.'

Lealholm to Egton Bridge

At Lealholm the path rejoins the river Esk and the railway, moving easily together on down the valley. As I cross a field at Underpark Farm a cockerel makes a run at me before deciding I'm not worth it and ushering his harem of five away from me.

A couple of times the path fords the river. There are footbridges, but I like to imagine that – at the height of summer – I'd take my boots off and wade across. I imagine Nicholas Postgate performing surreptitious baptisms in such places.

The approach to Carr End is a lovely stretch of the walk on that packhorse route, the stones winding through woodland where the bluebells and wild garlic carpet the ground. The river runs fast between sheer rock walls, properly alert now in contrast to its lazy spell upstream, and crashes over great sharp-sided boulders.

Egton Bridge

A memorial stone to 'Nicholas Postgate, Priest and Martyr' stands beside the river as you enter the village of Egton Bridge.

The inscription reads: 'Kirk-dale House was his birth-place and childhood home and there is a strong tradition that its site lies between this stone and the River Esk.'

The house was destroyed long ago, but Postgate is still cherished here. At St Hedda's Catholic church they hold mementos of him including his tabernacle, rosary, crucifix and chalice. A stained-glass window depicts him striding across the moor, bent into the wind, his grey hair flying (**photo opposite**). Just beyond the church is the pub. Once called the Railway Hotel, it's now The Postgate Inn in his honour and is the perfect place for an overnight stop.

In the 1830s, one of Postgate's long-forgotten secret churches was discovered hidden in the roof of a cottage in the village, still known as The Mass House. There was a look-out in the thatch, and an escape route through which Postgate could flee into the woods.

Egton Bridge to Whitby

Next morning the packhorse route is replaced by a wide, well-graded but untarmacked road all the way to Grosmont. A sign on a house explains that this is

'Barnard's Road Toll', and lists prices: 4d for a horse and two wheeled cart. From Grosmont it is a gentle climb over the fields and past a string of handsome stone farmhouses before dropping back down to the next valley village, Sleights.

Around Sleights I get back on the packhorse route, its faintly glowing stones leading me on from field to field and through the woods via the final village, Ruswarp, all the way to the outskirts of Whitby. I marvel at the effort that went into its construction, about the many builders, the organisation, the act of hauling each of these great stones miles out across open country to establish an all-weather route to town.

I'm straining for a view of St Hilda's Priory at Whitby – and the sea – and finally, at Hagg House, I get my reward. What a beacon it must have been to medieval man. Would it evoke awe, or reverence? I am thinking of Caedmon who, in his own way, is as significant a figure as Nicholas Postgate. Postgate was a humble village lad who became a great pastor, Caedmon was a shepherd who became a great Christian poet, the first English poet whose name we know.

Whitby

Whitby and Whitby Abbey

I arrive in Whitby, the harbour filled with boats. After two days soaked in nature, I am startled to hear the clatter of a town going about its business. The final hundred yards of this pilgrimage are the most challenging: a pounding climb up the 199 steps to St Mary's church and the ruins of the Norman abbey, but worth it for the view alone. The cliff-top abbey replaced Hilda's 7th century monastery but was destroyed by Henry VIII in 1538. As if Henry's efforts weren't enough, in 1914 the abbey was shelled by German battlecruisers causing considerable further damage, although their target had apparently been the

coastguard station at the end of the headland. At the top of the steps, in a corner of St Mary's churchyard, a stone cross has stood since 1898: Caedmon's Cross. I perch on its plinth and look out across the town.

The 8th century chronicler Bede tells Caedmon's story in his *Ecclesiastical History of the English People*. Caedmon lived at the abbey in about 680, while St Hilda was abbess. Bede describes him as a lowly layman 'well advanced in years' with no artistic leanings, who would never join in when others sang songs after supper. One night a man appeared in his dreams and asked him to sing about the creation. He told the man he was unable to, but

ST HILDA AND THE HEADLESS STONE SNAKES

St Hilda, more correctly St Hild, was an Anglo-Saxon princess and abbess of Whitby Abbey who, in 664, hosted the Synod of Whitby, an event as significant for faith in this country as the Reformation would be 900 years later. At this synod the king of Northumbria decreed that, in his kingdom, Easter would in future be calculated, and monastic rules determined, according to the customs of Rome, rather than those of the Irish monks at Iona which had been observed until that time. Thus, Celtic Catholicism was abandoned in the kingdom, in favour of Roman Catholicism.

Significant stuff. However, locally, St Hilda was more appreciated for banishing the snakes which, according to the Snakeshead Legend, plagued the town. St Hilda invoked the Gospel of St Mark and spoke Christ's words: 'Be removed and cast into the sea.' First she prayed for the power to remove the snakes' heads, then to turn their bodies to stone. As proof, headless stone snakes – or, as we might prefer to call them, ammonites – were discovered all over the place. In Victorian times, Whitby souvenir hawkers would carve snakes' heads onto ammonites to sell to tourists.

then found himself singing songs in praise of God the creator which, Bede says, 'he had never heard before'. It became apparent that Caedmon could hear a piece of scripture and immediately turn it into verse. When Hilda learned of his gift she declared it divine. Little of Caedmon's poetry survives, but Bede quotes the words of the poem he learned to sing in his dream. It is one of the earliest pieces of English poetry and reads, in modern English:

'Praise we the fashioner now of Heaven's
    fabric,
The majesty of his might and his mind's
    wisdom,
Work of the world-warden, worker of all
    wonders,
How he the Lord of Glory everlasting
Wrought first for the race of men Heaven
    as a roof-tree,
Then made the Middle Earth to be their
    mansion.'

As I wander on to take in the abbey ruins I think of the theme that has emerged on this pilgrimage: of seemingly very ordinary people who achieve remarkable things.

Left: The cliff-top ruins of Whitby Abbey and (**above**) Caedmon's Cross.

19

In the footsteps of St Cuthbert, St Oswald and St Aidan

Seahouses to Holy Island, Northumberland

From the home of the kipper, via a king's castle and a saint's cave, then over the causeway to the most important medieval cultural, artistic and religious site in Northern England

I am enjoying two inspiring prospects as I stand beside the harbour at Seahouses. One is out to sea, where the Farne Islands lie low in the water. The other, along the coast to the north and beyond an enticing stretch of silver-blonde sand, is of the barley-sugar stone of Bamburgh Castle, standing imperiously atop a molar of sheer-sided rock.

These prospects would, I admit, be even brighter if the weather were fine, but today happens to be one of rain: the sort of rain that makes up for in persistence what it lacks in drownability. I started my first pilgrimage with the thought that into every pilgrim's life a little good fortune must fall. Now, beginning my nineteenth, I concede that a little rain must inevitably fall into it too.

No matter. I will not let it detract from my enjoyment of the wonderful, contrasting landscapes my route will take me through over the next two days: from islands teeming with birdlife, via a glorious Northumberland beach, to rugged moorland, forests and valleys. And then will come the highlight: the eerie, alien experience of walking over the seabed to Holy Island, historically known as Lindisfarne.

The lives of three great Northern saints intertwine on this walk, all of them intimately associated with Holy Island and the route I shall follow. Although the route from Seahouses is mainly on St Oswald's Way, St Cuthbert walked here too. Along the route I pick up a part of St Cuthbert's Way, and visit a forest cave associated with him. Then there is St Aidan, founder of the monastery that is my final destination. Aidan is buried at Bamburgh, in the shadow of the castle, in a church dedicated to him. So I have three saints to guide me on this journey: a level of protection few pilgrimages can offer.

View across to Inner Farne Island from the beach near Seahouses.

PRACTICAL INFORMATION

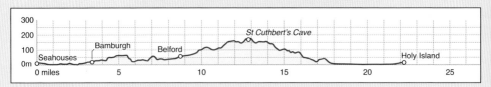

- **Terrain** A mix of beach walking and footpaths over fields and moorland
- **Difficulty** Moderate
- **Directions & GPS*** 019.pdf, 019.gpx, 019.kml at 🖳 https://trailblazer-guides.com/press

  * See p10-11 for more information on downloads

ROUTE OVERVIEW   22.2 miles (35.7km)

Walking along sandy beaches and through dunes and fields, following the route of St Oswald's Way, in some places your exact route will be influenced by the tide. The walk culminates in a causeway crossing only accessible at low tide so it's important to check the tide times before you set out.

Seahouses to Belford   8.8 miles (14.2km)

WARNING! When you reach the point where the route crosses a major railway line, you will need to phone the signal box to check it is safe before crossing the line.

- **Time** 3 hours actual walking time
- **Total Ascent** 120m/393ft
- **Map** OS Explorer *340 Holy Island & Bamburgh*

Begin by walking along the beach, or over the sand dunes, for **3.3 miles** to Bamburgh, then alongside the B1342 for **1 mile**, before following St Oswald's Way overland. The route, generally well marked, runs over gently undulating farmland for **4.5 miles** to Belford.

Belford to Lindisfarne   13.4 miles (21.5km)

WARNING! Check the safe crossing times for the Lindisfarne causeway before setting out. See 🖳 holyislandcrossingtimes.northumberland.gov.uk

- **Time** 5 hours actual walking time
- **Total Ascent** 430m/1476ft,
- **Map** OS Explorer *340 Holy Island & Bamburgh*

Today's walk is all on St Oswald's Way, apart from one short diversion. The route runs over pasture for **2 miles** to Swinhoe Farm, then rises gradually through woodland to emerge on rough moorland and reach St Cuthbert's Cave after a further **2.1 miles**. From there, after retracing your steps for half a mile, you begin a long gentle descent through woodland, reaching Fenwick in **3.7 miles**. From here, it is **2.3 miles** to the causeway across to Holy Island, and a further **3.5 miles** to reach Lindisfarne Priory.

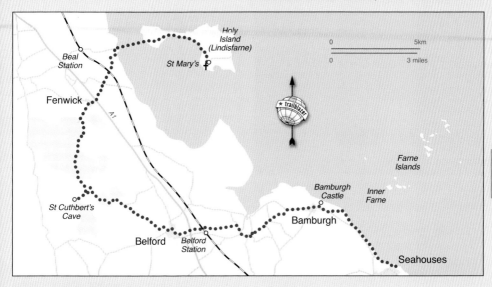

Day walk options

● **By public transport** Take the train to Chathill station, then a taxi to the start of the walk at Seahouses or Belford. To return to the mainland from Holy Island there is a mini-bus service in the summer (run by Woody's Taxis; ☎ 01289 547009, 💻 berwickupon tweedtaxis.co.uk), or call a taxi.

● **Taxi back to mainland** Knight's Taxis (☎ 07760-751667, 💻 knightstaxi.com).

Where to eat or stay along the way

● **Seahouses Stay** the night before your walk at the *Olde Ship Inn* (☎ 01665-720200, 💻 seahouses.co.uk/theoldeship, Main St NE68 7RD), a friendly pub perched above the harbour, then pick up a **picnic** lunch at Seahouses Co-Op on Main St before your boat trip to the Farne Islands.

● **Belford Stay** at the *Blue Bell Hotel* (☎ 01668-213543, 💻 bluebellhotel.com, Market Place), an old coaching inn that welcomes walkers.

PILGRIMAGE HIGHLIGHTS

● **Bamburgh** St Oswald's *Bamburgh Castle* (💻 bamburghcastle.com; 10am-5pm) and St Aidan's church (💻 staidan-bamburgh.co.uk; 10am-5pm; Radcliffe Rd).

● **Seek out** the hidden *St Cuthbert's Cave*.

● **Navigate** the tidal causeway to **Holy Island** (Safe crossing times: 💻 holyisland crossingtimes.northumberland.gov.uk).

● **Visit** *Lindisfarne Priory* (💻 english-heritage.org.uk/visit/places/lindisfarne-priory; usually 10am-5pm depending on tide times), the Holy Island home to St Cuthbert and St Aidan.

19

ST OSWALD – WARRIOR KING

Oswald was King of Northumbria from 634 until he died about eight years later, and was venerated in the Middle Ages. He spread Christianity across his kingdom, bringing the Irish monk Aidan from the Scottish Holy island of Iona and establishing him on Lindisfarne. Bede regarded Oswald as a saintly king, citing his generosity to the poor and to strangers, and saying he accompanied Aidan as he preached and translated his sermons into the local language for his congregations.

Oswald's Northumbrian kingdom dominated Britain in this period, and power was focused around his three palaces, one of them at Bamburgh. By giving Aidan Lindisfarne, Oswald enabled the monks of Iona to establish their monastery in the political heartland of his kingdom.

Oswald was killed in battle against the pagan Mercians at Oswestry – the name derived from Oswald's Tree – and miracles were said to follow his death. His relics were moved to various locations and subdivided many times, but his head found a home at Durham, visited on Walk 16, together with the remains of St Cuthbert.

Inner Farne

Inner Farne is not strictly a part of this walk, as you need to take a boat from Seahouses to get to it. Round trips take 3.5 hours, including an hour on the island and generally depart at around noon, from March to November (**photo left**).

I have planned this walk with just a three-hour trek on day one, so you do have time to take the boat, if you don't mind setting off for Belford in mid-afternoon. You may prefer to admire Inner Farne at a distance, and just get walking over that glorious beach to Bamburgh, but if you do go to the 16-acre island you will find it teeming with bird life. In summer, thousands of puffins, cormorants, shags, eider ducks and various varieties of tern nest here.

Apart from a lighthouse, all the buildings on the island are from the monastic period. As I wipe the salt spray from my face after the invigorating open-boat crossing and step on to the landing jetty, I come

Above: On the beach between Seahouses and Bamburgh with the castle (**below**) in the distance.

to the Fishehouse, on the site of the pilgrim hostelry built by Cuthbert. The Pele Tower, built to house the monks, is from 1540. Today, National Trust wardens live in it for nine months of the year.

The little church, from 1370, has a great stained-glass east window commemorating Cuthbert. This is a simple place, perfect for summoning the contemplative spirit before the briny boat trip back to the mainland.

Seahouses to Bamburgh

St Oswald's Way takes an unaccountable wander inland for this stretch, so I shun it to walk along the shore, wobbling a little as I shed my sea legs. With Northumberland's wonderful beaches at hand, why would you choose to walk in the fields? With the tide out, I can stride across the brown-sugar sands, over rock ramparts and limestone pavements pocked with pools teeming with miniature life, and within the sound of the waves' constant

Bamburgh Castle

rumble. If the wide beach were covered by the North Sea, a trail through the dunes would do just as well. For the final approach to Bamburgh I weave through the dunes, where the rain can't dampen the fire of the swathes of bright poppies, or the yellow tree lupins (**right**).

Bamburgh

Bamburgh Castle was home to St Oswald, and the village church is the final resting place of St Aidan, to whom it is dedicated. According to Bede, the 7th century chronicler, Aidan built a wooden church outside the castle walls in 635 and died here in 652. The present church is a curious building, begun in the 12th century but with various additions in contrasting styles, as if several churches had been slotted together. Inside is a 19th century stone *reredos* (the ornamental screen behind the altar) depicting the Northern Saints, and a wooden beam against which Aidan is said to have rested as his life ebbed away.

Bamburgh to Belford

The path takes to the meadows soon after Bamburgh, and I swish through the wet grass along a path that is freshly mown, well-signposted: a joy to walk. The woods at Spindlestone Heughs throw an umbrella over me and I can take my hood down and listen to the rain patter on the leaf canopy.

On the approach to Belford I descend through a meadow in which two young

ST CUTHBERT

Cuthbert's story is tied to that of St Aidan, who founded the priory on Lindisfarne. As a 17-year-old shepherd at Melrose on the Scottish borders, where St Aidan had also established a monastery, Cuthbert had a dream, which he interpreted as a vision, and next day discovered that Aidan had died. He joined the monastery at Melrose and soon became its prior, later becoming prior at Lindisfarne in the 670s.

Cuthbert reformed the monastery so that its monks conformed to the religious practices of the Church in Rome, rather than the Irish traditions of Celtic Christianity. This was unpopular, and Cuthbert decided to leave and live as a hermit, which he did first on St Cuthbert's Island, just off Lindisfarne from the monastery, later moving to Inner Farne island, where he built a chapel. However, at King Oswald's insistence, he was made bishop of Lindisfarne in 685.

Cuthbert died in 687 and was buried in a shrine in the monastery church. Miracles attributed to him brought many pilgrims to the island. However, in 793 Viking raiders desecrated the monastery and, fearing further attacks, the monks left the island, taking Cuthbert's remains with them. For seven years they wandered, before settling in Chester-Le-Street. In 995 St Cuthbert's relics were moved again, and eventually enshrined at Durham Cathedral (see p194).

hares are playing tag to cross the main London-Edinburgh line, where I am instructed to phone the signal box and get the all clear before I cross. I'm glad I do, as despite hearing nothing as I pick up the handset, an express sighs past within seconds. Then comes the A1 – where I rather wish there was a phone to let me know when I'll find a break in the chain of lorries filing north and south – followed by a walk alongside Belford Burn to the village.

Belford is an old coaching stop, and once stood astride the Great North Road, but is now bypassed and untroubled by through traffic. Yet it still feels like a traveller's place, with its wide main street and clutch of inns, and it's the only point during this pilgrimage with facilities for walkers.

St Cuthbert's Cave

The rain is still with me on day two. But I'm used to it by now. Up here on the Kyloe Hills, Oswald's Way and Cuthbert's Way meet, and travel on together to Holy Island, but I leave them as I make a 1-mile diversion to St Cuthbert's Cave. It is well hidden. I don't discover it until it is almost beneath my feet, tucked in a dell amid a dense patch of woodland.

The *Anglo-Saxon Chronicle* records that, in 875 as the Danes ravaged Lindisfarne the monks took St Cuthbert's body and wandered with it for seven years. According to legend, this sandstone cave, where an overhanging rock creates a shelter 24m wide, 7m deep and 3m high, might have been among the places in which either the monks took shelter with their holy relic, or where Cuthbert himself lived as a hermit before moving to the Farne Islands.

I pause in its shelter, only slightly nervous that the roof is held up by a very slender pillar of sandstone, like a finger under a chin. It's cosy, there's even a little natural fireplace at one end. So many hundreds of dedications have been cut into the stone

Path to St Cuthbert's Cave (inset)

over the centuries that the walls of the cave wear a full-body tattoo of them. There are even memorials, one family in particular carving dedications to several generations of their departed.

I decide, in defiance of the rain, to use the cave's acoustics for a verse of John Bunyan's only hymn: *To Be A Pilgrim*, also known as *He Who Would Valiant Be*. The cave tannoys out my words:

Crossing over to Holy Island, you can take the pilgrim route (**top**) or follow the causeway (**above**). Check it's safe to cross.

> There's no discouragement
> Shall make him once relent
> His first avowed intent
> To be a pilgrim

Spirits raised, I press on, back over the tops where I get a rather hazy view of distant Holy Island through the misty rain, and down through Sheillow Wood and the hamlet of Fenwick. Descending all the time, I reach Fishers Back Rd on the final leg before the walk across the sands. A skylark takes off, rising as it sings a song it might have learned from an old dial-up internet connection, only more tuneful.

Crossing to Holy Island

There are two ways to the island: you can strike out across the sands, guided by a series of tall poles along the official pilgrim route, or you can follow the causeway. But you can do neither at high tide. It's vital to plan for a safe crossing (see p220). I choose the causeway.

For me, this expanse of singing sand is eerie enough without having to worry about sinking into it. Even with cars passing every so often, walking the causeway is a watery, wilderness experience. The wind seems to be in a low, moaning conversation with itself. I'd say it was humming in the wires, except there are no wires out here, so maybe it's communing with the spirits of the sands. As one shore sinks behind me, the dunes ahead don't appear to get any closer for quite some time, and I mutter a prayer for deliverance, which is duly granted. I give thanks as I climb over the lip of the sand dunes onto dry land, and make for the village.

Holy Island foreshore

Holy Island

At the heart of the village is the ruined, red-stone Norman priory. Alongside it is the 12th century church of St Mary, close to the rocky shore, overlooking the expanse of glinting sandbanks between island and mainland.

What I love most about Holy Island are its vibrant, living connections with its past. One of the treasures of this place is the sumptuously illuminated Lindisfarne Gospels, created here to mark the discovery that 11 years after St Cuthbert's death, miraculously, his body had not deteriorated.

In the Lindisfarne Heritage Centre, on Marygate, you can see an electronic version of the Gospels and turn the virtual pages on screen. Close by, the gospels live on in an even more tactile way. The Lindisfarne Gospels Garden, which began as an exhibit at the Chelsea Flower Show in 2003, features some of the plants from which the monks extracted dyes to colour their manuscripts: feverfew, sage, lichens, toadflax; berries such as bilberry, mulberry, blueberry, elderberry; plus honeysuckle, iris and celandine. The yellow wallflowers that colonise stone walls all over the island also thrive here.

I wander around. On the far side of the priory is the harbour, where the upturned hulls of old fishing boats have been converted into stores through the addition of double doors let into the stern. Beyond, Lindisfarne Castle stands on the shore like a child's sand-bucket creation just beginning to crumble from the wind and waves. To the south I get a view all the way back to yesterday morning, in the shape of the impressive bulk of Bamburgh Castle.

I decide to pop in to St Mary's. Parts of it are 7th century, predating the priory, and it is probably on the site of the original monastery founded by Aidan. Under the Normans the monks returned to establish a cell at Lindisfarne and, in this church, they placed an empty tomb at the point where Cuthbert's body was once buried. Despite his remains now being in Durham, this was still a sacred spot, attracting many pilgrims.

The most striking feature is the lifesize elm sculpture, called *The Journey*, of six monks carrying St Cuthbert's coffin. It reminds me what pilgrimage is all about.

Holy Island – Ruins of the priory (**left**), statue of St Aidan (**centre**), and St Mary's church (**right**).

19

20

St Andrew's Way

From Earlsferry to St Andrews

Following the glorious Fife coastline to St Andrews, where the shrine of the apostle made this Scotland's most important pilgrim destination

The tide is just on the turn and lapping back over the seaweed, raising an evocative odour of pure undiluted seaside that wafts in on the breeze. Here, the view is utterly dominated by sea and sky, which are like two thick slices of bread in a doorstep jam butty: the narrow crescent of houses that line the bay being the red-roofed jam in the middle.

I'm standing on Chapel Ness, a headland of tumbled sandstone, looking out from the ruins of a little cliff-top chapel. To my left is the village of Earlsferry, a name that tells you all you need to know. The earl (of Fife) established a ferry, probably in the 10th century, bringing pilgrims the seven miles across the Firth of Forth from North Berwick. From here they would have walked to St Andrews, many going overland, but others hugging this glorious coastline to take in the numerous points of pilgrimage along the way: saints' shrines, holy wells, and caves where hermits lived.

Today the Fife Coastal Path makes a beautiful walk for the modern pilgrim, taking you over a mixture of clifftop stretches, across sandy and rocky beaches, and passing through the chain of pretty fishing villages in this, the romantically named East Neuk of Fife.

Along the way you encounter a clutch of local saints: St Adrian, St Monan and St Fillan. There are various pilgrim routes that share the name St Andrew's Way, since pilgrims approached it from every direction. The one described here offers the very finest walking route to St Andrews.

Earlsferry

PRACTICAL INFORMATION

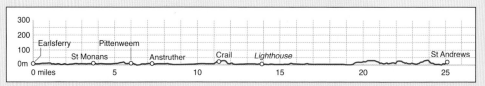

- **Terrain** A mix of coastal paths, sandy and rocky beaches, with steep ascents and descents, particularly towards the end of the walk
- **Difficulty** Challenging, with sections impassable at high tide
- **Directions & GPS*** 020pdf, 020.gpx, 020.kml at 🖥 https://trailblazer-guides.com/press
  * See p10-11 for more information on downloads

ROUTE OVERVIEW   25.1 miles (40.5km)

A challenging but spectacular coastal walk, following the Fife Coastal Path. It's important to plan ahead and be prepared for the sections that are impassable at high tide.

Earlsferry to Crail   11.4 miles (18.4km)

WARNING: At **high tide** the stretch between Newark Castle and St Monans, where it passes at the foot of the sea wall by St Monan's church, will be **under water**. A short **alternative inland route** is signposted just after Newark Castle which rejoins the coastal path just after the church, adding a negligible amount to the journey.

- **Time** 4 hours actual walking time   - **Total ascent** 300m/984ft
- **Map** OS Explorer *OL371 St Andrews & East Fife*

At Chapel Ness you immediately pick up the well-signed Fife Coastal Path all the way to St Andrews. The first **3.9 miles** to St Monan's run along the mainly level grassy clifftop. From St Monans the path is punctuated with lovely fishing villages, reaching Pittenweem after **1.7 miles**, Anstruther **1.6 miles** later and Crail after another **4.2 miles**.

Crail to St Andrews   13.7 miles (22.1km)

WARNING: At high tide two sections of the stretch beyond Fife Ness become **impassable**, and there are **no alternatives**. The first is 1.4 miles after Constantine's Cave, where the path runs along the beach for half a mile, passing beneath rocky cliffs and round a headland before returning above the high-tide line. The second comes shortly after passing the Torrance Golf Course, where the path again descends to the sands to pass beneath a rocky headland. **Check the tide times** before setting out: 🖥 metoffice.gov.uk/weather/ specialist-forecasts/ coast-and-sea/ beach-forecast-and-tide-times/gfn0h1ztx

- **Time** 5½ hours actual walking time   - **Total ascent** 548m/1798ft
- **Map** OS Explorer *OL371 St Andrews & East Fife*

In contrast to the previous day's landscape, this more rugged coastline has rocky headlands interposed with the occasional white-sand beach. The headland at Fife Ness is reached after **2.5 miles**, followed by a combination of cliff top and beach stretches, plus one short diversion inland, for the remaining **11.2 miles** to St Andrews.

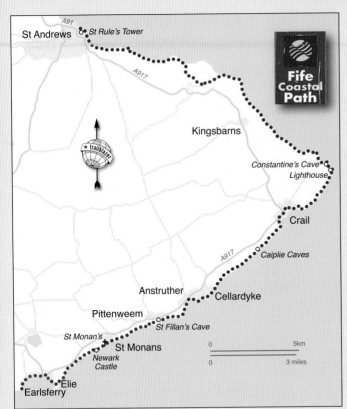

Day walk options

● **By public transport**
Markinch is the nearest railway station to the start at Earlsferry, while Leuchars station is closest to the end. Crail can be reached by bus or taxi from either station.

● **Taxi option** Markinch Cabs (☎ 01592-756550, 🖥 markinchcabs.co.uk); St Andrew's Quick Taxis (☎ 07938-151900, 🖥 stand rewsquicktaxis.co.uk).

Where to eat/stay

● **Elie** *Elie Bay Bed and Breakfast* (☎ 01333-330942, 🖥 eliebedand breakfast.co.uk, 2 Wadeslea KY9 1EB), close to the start of the walk.

● **Pittenweem Lunch** by the harbour, sampling the local seafood at either *The Dory Bistro & Gallery* (☎ 01333-311222, 🖥 thedory.co.uk, noon-2.30pm & 5-9pm, East Shore) or *Larachmhor Tavern* (☎ 01333-311888, 🖥 thelarachmhor.blogspot.com, 6 Midshore).
● **Crail Stay** in a historic fishing village at the characterful *Marine Hotel* (☎ 01333-450207, 🖥 crailbandb.co.uk, 54 Nethergate).

PILGRIMAGE HIGHLIGHTS

● Stunning coastal walking in the footsteps of St Adrian, St Monan and St Fillan.
● At Pittenweem explore **St Fillan's Cave** (Key from Cocoa Tree chocolate shop, High Street; 🖥 pittenweemchocolate.co.uk, Tue-Sun 10am-5pm).
● Watch out for guillemots, shag, eider, cormorants and dolphins as you walk through **Kilminning Coast Nature Reserve** (🖥 scottishwildlifetrust.org.uk).
● Explore the ruins of once-vast **St Andrew's Cathedral** and climb **St Rule's Tower**, built to house the saint's relics (🖥 historicenvironment.scot/visit-a-place/places/st-andrews-cathedral; Apr-Sept 9.30am-5.30pm; Oct-Mar 10am-4pm)

St Andrew's saint's day: 30 November

Earlsferry to St Monans

There is not much left of the Earlsferry chapel that welcomed so many medieval pilgrims – 15,000 in 1413 alone. Now there's just a gable-end and a rumpled blanket of grass covering the remaining low walls of the rest.

On the landward side, the chapel is flanked by Earlsferry Links, the first of an almost continuous string of golf courses that run right the way along the shore to my destination. You could probably hit a ball all the way to St Andrews without leaving a course.

I skirt the harbour, walking through Earlsferry, its little High Street lined with white – and in one case pink – cottages, and on through its twin village, Elie. I emerge on another headland, where a diminutive lighthouse stands, looking more like the ticket kiosk on a crazy-golf course than a housing for a life-saving light. I can't resist pausing again to take in the panorama of the Forth.

My path runs over a rugged clifftop and past several tumbledown ancient buildings, beginning with the ruined 13th century Ardross Castle with its looping chain of arches like a Loch Ness Monster in crumbling stone. Newark Castle comes next, striking an impressive silhouette on its honeycomb of sandstone. The cliff is crumbling too and has already pitched most of the castle into the sea.

St Monans

Right above the path on the cliff edge is the first pilgrim point: a church dedicated to the rather mysterious local saint, St Monan. His identity is uncertain but he may have been a Scottish saint killed here by Norse raiders, or an Irish bishop or missionary.

The church is a solid, foursquare place with a witch's-hat spire. In Monan's time this would have been a very simple building. The present church was built in the 14th century by the Scottish king David II, who came here on pilgrimage, praying for recovery from battle wounds. At the saint's intercession, the story goes, a barbed arrow that surgeons had failed to extract from his body miraculously released itself.

I step inside to find a bright, pure white space, the many windows flooding the building with light. A great 18th century model of a three-masted schooner hangs above the crossing, testament to the importance seafaring once had here. Today, just a few fishing boats dot St Monans' extensive harbour.

St Fillan's Cave, Pittenweem

Another village, another pilgrim point. Pittenweem comes from the Gaelic 'place of

Above: Newark Castle ruins, near St Monans.

Above: The 14th century church of St Monan.

the caves', the main cave being that of St Fillan. It is in an alley (**photo, right**), tucked beneath a bouffant arrangement of honeycomb-like sandstone, and protected by a handsome, cross-bearing gate. Once inside, a passageway cut into the stone slopes down into the earth, before opening out into a large, low cavern. A simple stone altar bears two vases of fresh-cut flowers, beside the spring and well named in St Fillan's honour. It's good to see the shrine is looked after so well. The cave was used by this Irish hermit saint as a chapel in the 8th century. Fillan was said to have miraculous healing powers, and a glowing arm, which he put to good use, using its light to write his sermons by.

Pilgrims on their way to St Andrews would stop at the cave, which was venerated for centuries after Fillan's death, and probably lived in by other hermits. After the Scottish Reformation (see p237) it became used in turn by smugglers, as a store for fishing nets, and a rubbish dump. In 1935 the shrine was cleared and reopened.

It is worth looking around Pittenweem when you pause for lunch. In the High St is the 14th century church, originally part of Pittenweem Priory, and the harbour is home to a fleet that specialises in harvesting fine Scottish shellfish: langoustine, lobsters, clams, crabs and scallops.

Anstruther and Cellardyke

Pittenweem is just a cliff top stroll, and a golf course, away from Anstruther and

On the path after Anstruther

Cellardyke, two villages that got rich on the herring trade. The name Cellardyke comes from Sil'erdykes, a reference to the shine of herrings' scales when they are hung in nets over walls (or dykes) to dry.

These and the other villages between St Monans and Crail feel like they are still real places, where fishing matters and tourism is a sideline.

Above: Caiplie Caves.

Caiplie Caves

From Cellardyke I pass through a caravan park and over the rough grass of the foreshore towards a pile of giant popcorn nuggets in sandstone. Marked on Ordnance Survey maps as The Coves and Hermit's Well, the Caiplie Caves are another ancient hermit residence. Hollowed out in the sandstone, the three caves are associated with St Adrian, an Irish monk who lived here until suffering martyrdom at the hands of heathen Viking raiders in 875. I peer into the largest, Chapel Cave. There are many crosses carved in its sandstone walls – some probably early Christian, others medieval, and reflecting the caves' importance to pilgrims – and two far older Pictish symbols: crescents or arches dating from the Late Iron Age and Early Medieval periods.

There are two other caves: Harmit's Cave, named after a 20th century hermit and said to have contained a stone bed, and Mortuary Cave, outside which human remains were discovered in 1841.

ST ANDREW

St Andrews is named after the fisherman who, with his brother Simon Peter, was called by Jesus to become an apostle, saying that he would make them 'fishers of men'. In 347, according to legend, St Rule brought Andrew's relics to a shrine that was established in the port of Kilrymont, which was renamed in the saint's honour.

The relics had been kept in a monastery at Patras, in Greece, but Rule, a monk there, was told by an angel in a dream to hide some of the bones, and later to take them to the ends of the earth for their protection. Legend has it he set sail with an odd assortment: a kneecap, an upper arm bone, three fingers and a tooth, but was shipwrecked off the coast of Fife. However, it is more likely that these relics were brought to Britain in 597 by Augustine, as part of his mission to Christianise Britain, and were brought on to Kilrymont in 732 by Bishop Acca of Hexham, a keen collector of religious relics. What he carried was literally priceless.

Because of the connection with the apostle, the town became the most important pilgrimage place in Scotland, and among the most popular in Europe. There has been a church in St Andrews since at least 747, and a cathedral since 1160. St Andrew's relics brought great wealth and political influence. All that stopped when pilgrimage ceased after the Scottish Reformation of 1559 (see p237).

The foreshore here is riven with prominent, dark-brown spines of stone, the vertebrae standing proud. A natural, shallow lagoon invites the cooling of pilgrim feet. As I walk on, a patch of yellow flag iris pinpoints the Hermit's Well. I look up the shallow cliff and see the fresh water sliding over a flat expanse of rock.

Crail

Crail is the most easterly of the coastal villages along the East Neuk of Fife, and quite possibly the most attractive. A good place to end your first day's walk.

Marketgate, at the medieval heart of the village, became the largest marketplace in Europe after Robert the Bruce granted the right to hold Sunday markets in 1310. Sabbath shopping went down very badly after the Reformation, and the Church of Scotland tried to have the market moved to a weekday. It failed. The parish church in Marketgate contains an 8th century cross-slab, dating from the times of the saints encountered on the walk.

The second day of walking is very different. There are no more pretty villages, and the coast becomes increasingly wild and solitary. The way is more rugged, the path fickle, at times on cliff tops, at others on the beach, often yo-yoing repeatedly between the two. There are points after Fife Ness you can't cross at high tide (see p230), so ensure you use the tide table to avoid getting stranded.

Now the golf courses are a constant presence. As a counterpoint, the grassland, saltmarsh and coastal scrub of the Scottish Wildlife Trust's reserve at Kilminning Coast brings you wild nature. It boasts nesting sites for whitethroats, stonechats and linnets. Offshore you might see guillemots, shag, eider, cormorants and dolphins.

As I round the rocky headland at Fife Ness, passing beneath its stubby little lighthouse and coastguard station, I realise

Crail

I have reached a turning point, quite literally. From here I am on the home straight to St Andrews.

Constantine's Cave

Beside the path as it skirts Balcomie Golf Course, tucked on the seaward side of a line of little white posts, is Constantine's Cave. Named after Constantine II, a 10th century king

Above: Buddo Rock and the path nearby.

of Scotland, this cave is a much simpler affair than Caiplie – not much more than two giant slabs of green, lichen-stained rock leaning against each other. The local legend is that the king was killed in or near the cave in a battle with the Danes in the 870s, but there is no hard evidence. There is, however, evidence of Christian activity: crosses cut into the rock, and carvings of animals, which date from 800 to 1000. During

the Celtic period it was probably a chapel or hermitage.

From here there are several miles of wild and remote Fife coastline; the perfect place for contemplation. The most prominent landmark on this final stretch, Buddo Rock, does not seem to have any religious significance, but the great, towering yet squat thing does have quite a presence.

Soon after Buddo I get my first sight of St Andrews: three tall thin towers, which seem to change shape and configuration as I approach. One looks like Big Ben for a while, then it becomes attached to a partner and morphs into a rocket at its launch pad.

St Andrews

There is a great deal of up and down on

Approaching St Andrews

this final stretch, before the path runs beside the city's sandy beach, crossing the entrance to the narrow harbour before a final sprint uphill to the once-mighty complex of cathedral and monastery.

The towers of stone I have been puzzling over from a distance begin to make sense close up. They turn out to be surviving pinnacles of the otherwise obliterated cathedral, and a 100ft tall square tower designed to act as a beacon to pilgrims coming to the shrine of St Andrew. This is St Rule's Tower, built in the 12th century to house the relics of St Andrew, and attached to St Rule's church, the precursor of the later cathedral. Climb its 156 steps and you are rewarded with spectacular views across this very well-ordered town, with its wide streets and stolid stone shops and houses, to the castle where the bishops lived.

As I look down at the ruins, I reflect that it was the mass of stone plundered at the Reformation from the vast cathedral, the largest church in medieval Scotland, that enabled such an elegant town to be built. Nevertheless, this surviving tower is still profoundly impressive, and moving. I can't think of a finer end to a pilgrimage than climbing up here at the end of such a spectacular coastal path.

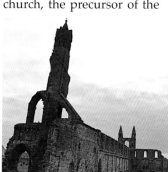

St Andrews Ruins of the cathedral (**left**), St Rule's Tower (**centre**) and gateway (**right**).

THE SCOTTISH REFORMATION

The Scottish Reformation of 1559 was a profound turning point in the nation's religious, political and cultural history. The break with the Church in Rome in 1560, as part of a wider European Protestant Reformation, marked the end of 500 years obedience to the Pope. Scotland developed a Presbyterian national church, founded by John Knox.

As in England, this Reformation brought about a concerted campaign to destroy every symbol of 'Popery': every piece of religious architecture, art and sculpture associated with the Church in Rome. The differing ways the reformed churches in England, Scotland and Ireland developed brought about decades of conflict in what was known as the War of the Three Kingdoms.

INDEX